WHO IS A DANDY?

WHO IS A DANDY?

by

GEORGE WALDEN

ON DANDYISM AND GEORGE BRUMMELL

JULES BARBEY D'AUREVILLY

translated
by
George Walden

GIBSON SQUARE BOOKS

This first edition first published in 2002

Gibson Square Books Ltd
15 Gibson Square
London N1 0RD
tel: +44 (0)20 7689 4790
fax: +44 (0)20 7689 7395
publicity@gibsonsquare.com
www.gibsonsquare.com

UK and European Distribution & Sales by:
Turnaround Publishers Services
3 Olympia Trading Estate
Coburg Road
London UK N22 6TZ
tel: +44 (0)20 8829 3000
fax: +44 (0)20 8881 5088
orders@turnaround-uk.com
www.turnaround-uk.com

International sales and permissions contact:
Gibson Square Books Ltd in London

ISBN 1-903933-18-8

Typesetting by Perseus
Printed by Bookwell Ltd

For Sarah, whose help and advice have been invaluable, as always.

ACKNOWLEDGEMENTS

I am grateful to Bryan Appleyard, Georges Liébert and Freddie Raphael for our discussions about dandyism in ancient and modern guise, and for reading my text. Of the authors I have read, I would like to single out Stephen Bayley for the ideas contained in his always stylish and illuminating books and articles. Also *Masculin Singulier: Le Dandysme et son Histoire*, by Marylène Delbourg-Delphis (Hachette, 1985).

WHO IS A DANDY?

WHO IS A DANDY?

Some time in the 1830s, in the town of Caen in Normandy, a young Frenchman caught sight of an unlikely figure: an imperious Englishman dressed in tattered clothes. The mask-like hauteur of his face and his air of ruined elegance made a startling impression. The spectacle was the more remarkable since the man was emerging from the modest burg's smartest hotel, the Hôtel d'Angleterre. For all his shabbiness not all remnants of respectability were gone. In his soiled waistcoat and patched trousers, retrieved from a tailor that morning, there were echoes of a former splendour, and unusually in those post-revolutionary times he was wearing a wig. It did little to rescue his dignity. The thing sat crooked on his head, leaking sticky rivulets where he had oiled it too assiduously.

From long habit he bowed when he met a lady of his acquaintance, though he was careful not to raise his hand to his head in salutation for fear of upsetting the (already crazy) angle of the wig. To complete the impression of senility his jaw worked soundlessly as he walked.

From time to time he veered towards a building or the street, close to toppling; a man held upright by little more, it seemed, than stiff-necked pride. The effect was both grotesque and affecting. Yet except for mocking children passers-by scarcely spared him a glance. They had grown used to the sight of the town's mendicant celebrity, and had long ceased marvelling at his precipitous decline.

Within the space of a few years the most pernickety dresser the town had seen had come down from three changes of linen per day to this beggarly state. The turning point had been when his once immaculate starched cravat in cambric became so soiled and spotted with snuff he had taken to wearing a black silk handkerchief at his neck. Till recently he would never have been seen without his primrose gloves; now that his once handsome hands would have benefited from covering, they were bare to the world. As for his boots, formerly polished to a dazzling sheen, not just the uppers but the under-soles, they too were scuffed and holed. Worst of all, he stank. As the staff at the Hôtel d'Angleterre knew too well, the disintegrating Englishman had only intermittent control of his bowels.

Had the Frenchman followed him he would have seen more distressing sights. The dotard's first stop was a boulangerie where, as ever, he requested a couple of his favourite *biscuits de Rheims*. He made no move to pay, nor did *le patron* make any demand for money. Instead he handed him his biscuits, though this time without a smile; he was starting to tire of his distinguished sponger and would soon insist on cash, obliging him to pawn a watch chain or treasured snuff box to buy his daily treat. For now the Englishman repaid his generosity silently, with a bow whose condescension and old-world graciousness were clearly in his opinion payment enough.

Next the scarecrow honoured a café with his presence. It was the kind of establishment of which he had often spoken in horror, where folk of modest origins drank, smoked and spat. He was thirsty for a second coffee, and without a single franc in his pocket. The hotel, wise to his tricks, allowed him a single cup, and there was nowhere except the café who would give him tick. Again, *la patronne* was rewarded with a bow; she would not see her money till after his death. Next on his list of charitable tradesmen was the pharmacist, but here he was out of luck, and the owner made it clear that he had come to the end of his line of credit. The Englishman departed the shop nose in the air, but without his much-needed bottle of eau de cologne.

Had the Frenchman encountered him some time earlier at the Hôtel d'Angleterre, he might have witnessed a still more poignant scene. On certain evenings the Englishman had been in the habit of throwing soirées in his suite. Like his wig they were something from another era, and though his clothes were already threadbare he was got up for the occasion in a way no one ever dressed in provincial France: in trousers like hose that showed off still comely legs, a black waistcoat and superb blue coat with gold buttons. Flowers and candles had been deployed in his room, and at eight o'clock sharp a waiter, primed for the task, threw open the door and announced the Duchess of Devonshire. As the names rang out and he welcomed his guests, members of the hotel staff watched, awestruck. Dukes, Lords, Royalty even ...

The host appeared to be everywhere, greeting his guests with exquisite bows and murmured amiabilities, taking ladies by the arm to escort them into the interior of the room, circulating amongst the illustrious figures with an air of practised grace and tranquil pride. Then, when the soirée was at its height, the smiling mask would fall from his face. Suddenly he would collapse, weeping, into a chair. The England whose flower of fashion he had welcomed existed only in his mind. The soirées were a fantasy, the grand names no more than ghosts. There was no Lord Yarmouth, no Lord Alvanley, no Lady Connyngham, and most certainly no Prince of Wales, in fact no flesh-and-blood guests at all. And not even anyone to play their parts. Only the down-at-heel Englishman acting out his lonely charade. He never got through his receptions without reality breaking in, robbing him of his anguished illusions, and it was a mercy when the waiter, promptly at ten, announced the phantom carriages.

Since then things had gone from bad to worse. The elegant Englishman had let himself go entirely. He had lost his figure, then his hair, then his self-respect, and finally his self-control: he became an obese loon in tattered clothes who snatched the best food from fellow residents at the hotel, or sprawled in the street. Finally he went mad and was committed. His personal habits had become disgusting but the nuns at the hospice of the Bon Sauveur looked after him well, and he rallied a little in their care. But this was the end. The crazy old Regency Beau whose custom it had been to spend the first half of the day at his toilet and the second in gaming or at balls had fallen into indigence and idiocy. Beau Brummell, prince of fashion and autocratic ruler of the Age of Elegance, whose gambling debts had made him an exile in France, ended his days in moral and physical degradation, a bedlamite fouling himself in his asylum.

The young Frenchman who had caught sight of him in Caen was Jules-Amédée Barbey d'Aurevilly, a minor provincial noble, later to become a famous novelist and critic. We do not know exactly when he saw him, but whenever it was that glimpse of the greatest dandy of all time must have lodged firmly in his memory. It was Barbey who was to produce *Du Dandysme et de George Brummell*, the most penetrating and original study of dandyism ever written.

If three things sum up our age they are science and technology, neo-liberal economics, and an infatuation with fashion and style. To understand the science you must know something of Darwin, and to understand economics you must be acquainted with the theories of Adam Smith. For a fuller understanding of the importance of style and fashion in our lives, and of the instincts on which they rest, Barbey's essay is essential.

Here is a tract written in 1844 that remains not just relevant to our day, but in some respects in advance of our age. It is a startlingly modern document. Barbey's theory of elegance is one of those rare works that can be read either backwards or forwards in time. A colourful interpretation of the Regency period, it also helps to explain things we may not have fully understood about the hedonism and style-consciousness of twenty-first-century England. The cult of celebrity, preoccupation with appearance, the new dandyism amongst men, the importance of "attitude", the studied ironies of the post-modernist era — all have their fore-echo in this astonishingly precocious work.

A modern message leaps from the page. What could be more suggestive of our era than his description of Brummell as possessing "A cold langour ... Eyes glazed with indifference ... A concentrated irony ... The boldness of conduct, the sumptuous impertinence, the preoccupation with exterior effects, with vanity incessantly present."? There is no avoiding the term: in today's parlance Brummell would be "cool".

Then as now there was no lack of Grundyish voices to deplore excessive concern with style and fashion. "Topmost evanescent froth" was Thomas Carlyle's judgment on clothes in *Sartor Resartus*, a decade after the Age of Elegance had closed and a few years before the Victorian era began. For him dandyism was "a survival of the primeval superstition, self-worship". "Dandyism is a modish affectation," Balzac chimed in at about the same time, in his *Traité de la Vie Elégante*. "When he makes himself into a dandy a man becomes a piece of boudoir furniture, a cleverly contrived tailor's dummy who can be placed on horseback or on a sofa, and can bite or suck the end of his cane, but a thinking creature — never!"

Barbey disagreed. His essay is no drear sermon against vanity and ephemera. For him the refinement of fashion and Regency manners were not intimations of decadence, but the sign of a golden age. Far from denouncing dandyism's excesses, he legitimised them. Far from despising vanity and frivolity he saw them as a positive force in human affairs. Barbey gave dandyism an almost spiritual status: "Dandies are as eternal as caprice. Humanity has as much need of their attractions as of its most imposing heroes, of its most austere grandeurs."

The fact that this inversion of conventional morality was inspired by our own Beau Brummell makes it the more remarkable that his essay is so little known in the country of his hero's birth. Tales of Brummell's life have been lovingly recounted by generations. There remains some dispute about the exact number of people it took to make his gloves (it is said that one tailor looked after the thumb), but we know of his insistence that cravats must be starched, that his shirts were taken to the countryside to be laundered, of his invention of what proved to be the forerunner of stretch pants, and of the rumour (apocryphal?) that his boots were cleaned in champagne. We marvel at the exquisiteness (or fatuity) of his manners, but also at his legendary capacity for impertinence, not least towards his one-time friend and patron, the Prince Regent. And we read with sneaking sympathy (or with secret satisfaction) of the great dandy's downfall from arbiter of fashion of an entire era into debt, exile and insanity. But these are mere externals. For a more radical understanding of what Brummell and his kind signified we must look to people like Barbey or Baudelaire. The English invented dandyism, the French explained it.

Barbey, whose horror of Puritanism pervades his work, does not see the rise and fall of George Bryan Brummell as a morality tale. His essay paints a brilliant psychological portrait, and is concerned with far more than the fashions of a bygone era. What excites him is not so much the thought of the Great Dandy at his toilet, or the well-worn anecdotes, as the idea of dandyism as a creed, a religion which supplies its own ethic and aesthetic, its philosophy of life.

Du Dandysme must be the only treatise on a fundamental aspect of human nature that began as an article for a fashion journal. Its origins can be traced to a piece destined for *Le Moniteur de la Mode*, a sort of contemporary *Vogue* magazine. Expanded into a small book it helped focus attention on dandyism in France. There it was to become more of a literary than a social concept, one that was to influence a succession of authors, from Baudelaire through Huysmans and Mallarmé to Proust, whose Baron Charlus has something of the Brummell about him. Baudelaire planned to write a study, but after reading Barbey's essay he gave the idea up, on the grounds that his friend had said it all, and confined himself to an article (unpublished in his time) which echoed some of Barbey's more elevated views: "Dandyism is the last spark of heroism amidst decadence ... Dandyism is a sunset. Like the declining day-star it is glorious, without heat and full of melancholy."

How a minor French writer, who was treated as an eccentric in his day (his stock is currently rising), was inspired by an English man of fashion to produce a small classic is a historical curiosity in itself. One explanation is that in the post-Napoleon period Anglomania was in the air. First it was Byron (a dandy himself, declaring that Napoleon took second place to Brummell) who captured the French imagination. Then Carlyle inadvertently heightened their interest in dandyism by his praise of heroes. Barbey's hero was Brummell, the ageing dandy he had glimpsed in Caen in his youth, and whom he saw as incarnating the spirit of a superior age.

Historically the Englishman and the Frenchman belonged to successive generations, yet their lives overlapped in suggestive ways. George Bryan Brummell was born in 1778, the son of a government clerk who had profited by becoming the private secretary of Lord North. Prime Minister from 1770 to 1782, North was known as the "God of emoluments", and the £30,000 fortune the Dandy was to inherit and dissipate had been built up thanks to his Lordship's free-handedness with his perks. The trajectory of the young Brummell was a model for socially aspiring young men of the times, and to an extent still is today. Though his father had once been in commerce, the boy was sent to Eton, where he made the necessary friends, then to Oxford, where academic studies did not detain him long. The next step up for this most unmilitary of men was a commission in the best of regiments, the 10th Hussars. There his stylishness and lively character attracted the eye of the lumpish Prince Regent, whose friend he became and whose dandyish aspirations he tutored and encouraged.

It was not long before the unlikely soldier abandoned his commission in favour of his true vocation: a life of elegance, idleness, gambling and drinking. His career as man about town and foremost social celebrity of Regency England lasted an astonishing two decades, from 1794 to 1816. In matters of taste and style, as Barbey observes, it was the Prince Regent who was courtier to Brummell, not the other way round. An addict of immoderation in everything but sex, he allowed celebrity to go to his head. Risqué mockery of the Regent's mistress, Mrs Fitzherbert, ended with the Prince cutting his old friend publicly, whereupon Brummell took his famous revenge. Ignored by the Prince at a public encounter, Brummell retaliated by asking an acquaintance to whom the Regent had spoken, "Who's your fat friend?" Thereafter his fortunes began to wane, and gambling debts finally drove him across the Channel. For fourteen years he kept up his end as the "King of Calais", on whom the English nobilty en route to Paris were pleased to pay a call; then, when the debts piled up and poverty gripped him, as the British Consul in Caen, a sinecure tossed to him by his old friends. It was a job whose meagre emoluments he was glad to accept but whose scarcely existent functions he felt himself too superior to fulfil.

At the time of Brummell's death Barbey, born in Caen in

1808, was thirty-two. His Norman background was significant in that it made him feel a (somewhat fanciful) affinity with the English, and as the over-exuberant lists of Dukes and Lords in his essay show, particularly with the English aristocracy; at heart Barbey was a romantic reactionary. After studying law he left Caen for Paris, where he had spent two years as a student, to become a writer and journalist. He made slow progress, and it was only in the mid-1840s, when he was thirty-seven, that he penetrated the Parisian literary world. As an author he led a scabrous existence peppered with scandals: his works (such as *Le Bonheur dans Le Crime,* in *Les Diaboliques,* in which the hero and his mistress murder the man's wife and live happily ever after) were seen as amoral and frequently landed him in court on charges of libel or obscenity. A right-wing anarchist and fiery polemicist, he could also be a discerning critic, and was to be one of the loudest defenders of Baudelaire's *Les Fleurs du Mal.*

If the overstatement, perverse logic, startling aphorisms and occasional obscurity of his essay sometimes read like the youthful infatuation of a spirited but wayward mind, we should remember that Barbey was a dandy himself, of the more flamboyant type: he favoured flaming colours, flared coats, a red cape, a Spanish nobleman's hat, and a dagger. All this despite the insistence in his essay that true dandyism, like true originality, was an English monopoly. Like Baudelaire he styled himself an "écrivain-dandy", even though the idea of the writer-dandy was anomalous in his own terms: the writer's works are written to endure, whereas his own philosophy of dandyism was based on its ephemerality and inutility. But then Barbey was not a man to shy away from self-contradiction.

Barbey produced his famous essay after writing several minor novels in his early twenties. Later he was to dismiss it, with uncharacteristic modesty, as a "bauble", "a little nothing" written for his own amusement and for that of a few friends. The truth is that Barbey was proud of it, and with reason. Half jeu d'esprit, half in earnest, it is a work whose power of psychological analysis he never bettered. Barbey dissected vanity with the same icy truthfulness as Choderlos de Laclos, in *Les Liaisons Dangereuses*, had laid bare cold-hearted and predatory love.

Du Dandysme appeared in 1845. The timing was politically significant. At the turn of the century France had still been largely composed of peasants and artisans; after the final defeat of Napoleon a working class began to emerge. The conflict of 1848 between the now dominant bourgeoisie and the new proletariat was brewing, and socialism was in fashion. Barbey greeted the advent of a mercantile era with patrician distaste. A preface to a second edition of his essay in 1879 is frank about his state of mind: the god of Progress, he wrote, was turning human beings into "a race of vermin." Elevated souls such as Brummell would have had no place in a society where the very idea of anyone being different to anyone else made people gnash their teeth: "people hate originality like a title of nobility."

In England, Progress had advanced with swifter, iron-footed steps. The Regency was long over and Barbey's other heros — Fox, Sheridan, Shelley, Byron — had gone. The Industrial Revolution was transforming society and in 1837, seven years before his essay, Queen Victoria had ascended the throne. For Barbey England had passed its zenith. Brummell had been a fleeting star in a darkening firmament and the country was destined to return to its familiar condition of "hypocrisy and spleen." Now a less attractive England would assert itself, as the country reverted to type: "The spark of intelligence of its greatest men had shone for a single moment on this country of arrogant Pharisaism, of glacial and mendacious convention, where the mummy of formality and religious sentiment still reigns in the depths of its whitened sepulchre."

In today's terms the minor provincial noble, whose title was rather recent and who had adopted the name of an uncle for effect, would be seen as a young fogey and reactionary snob. He appears to have looked back on Brummell as the supreme representative of a gilded era in a country which had never suffered the Revolution and in whose social life aristocratic values had been given their rightful place. Yet as always it would be a mistake to interpret a gifted author in solely political terms. Writers of Barbey's talent can be spurred to extraordinary insights for dubious motives, and the passion and impetuousness with which his essay was written led him to transcend the confines of his subject.

His bravura and epigrammatic style, themselves directed against the democratising grain of the times, match the originality of his perceptions. The result is edgy, spirited, provocative, sometimes outrageous. His emotional engagement with his subject gives the work an extraordinary intensity — a fanaticism almost — in which paradox is occasionally transmuted into profundity. It would be easy, but pointless, to accuse him of impudence and extravagance for constructing an entire theory of life around a single individual. The fact is that subject and author were ideally matched, and in each of them impudence and extravagance were not aberrations, they were the point.

This congenital intemperance made Barbey of limited use as a fashion critic. Drawn to ideas and preferring a high style, he failed to strike the right note between abstract speculation and the journalistic tone preferred by *Le Moniteur de la Mode*. The article which was to become a book was published in 1843 under the pseudonym of Maximilien de Syrène, and was his first attempt to elaborate a theory of style.

Entitled "On Elegance", it took issue with Montesquieu for failing to come to grips with the question of taste (he had shrugged it off as nothing more than a "je ne sais quoi"). On the contrary, Barbey reproved the author of *L'Esprit des Lois*, those concerned with fashion and style were true artists, and elegance had its place in the world. "More than grace but less than beauty, it is composed of both beauty and grace. Why, for example, should the notion of beauty not be realised in little things and elevated, thanks to grace, above the simple idea of prettiness?"

Beauty was imposing and intoxicating, elegance had the advantage of being "more amiable." It was also a discipline, and you had to work at it. As an example he gave the Austrian Prince of Kaunitz, who spent a part of each morning passing through successive rooms while four valets, positioned for the purpose, blew scented powder over his wig in order to arrive at exactly the right nuance.

At the end of his article Barbey announced that a follow-up piece would appear shortly. It never did. As he admitted later, "The commercial interests who owned the magazine thought that I wrote in too metaphysical a way, too high-flown for their public ..." The author himself was discontented with his work, feeling that his ideas and formulations had been smothered in the tone of "false chattiness" required by the magazine. Fired with enthusiasm to develop his theme he left *Le Moniteur* and announced to a friend his decision to write a biographical article on Brummell.

Now "le grand Brummell" took centre stage. Barbey had become obsessed by dandyism, and it was natural that he should focus on a man who had characterised the creed in all its grandiose absurdity. The trouble was that, apart from that glimpse of him in Caen during the writer's youth, he knew little about him. Discovering that there were few books or articles on the theme, he wrote to Captain William Jesse, an Englishman who was preparing a life of Brummell, begging him for material. He emphasised the need for the maximum of external detail: "When we are talking of Brummell, even the way he cut his nails is important."

Receiving a helpful response, in a fury of inspiration he began writing in January 1844, certain he could complete the whole thing in a matter of days. By 29 February, "my pen still smoking", he had finished.

In April he received Jesse's book. He thought it pedestrian and long-winded, which it was, and his idea of gratitude to the author who had gone out of his way to help him was to describe Jesse in his essay as "this admirable chronicler who does not forget enough." What Barbey had planned as a biographical piece had developed into a scintillating work of theory. Nevertheless, insofar as he was concerned with the facts, Jesse's book obliged him to revise a few points. By July he was satisfied with his work, telling a friend excitedly that "I think the general ideas are remarkable. As for the rest, you will see ..." He had hoped to have it printed in the prestigious literary magazine *La Revue des Deux Mondes*, but it turned him down. ("Too much originality", Barbey complained sardonically.)

It was published in a small edition in early 1845 and was read mainly by friends. "It was circulated amongst a few people from hand to hand", he wrote in the preface to the second edition, "a form of intimate and abstruse publicity that appears to have brought it luck." Reviews were few, and frequently critical. He was accused of an affectation of profundity and of writing in an over-licked style. "At least I am called names I like (and that women like too)," he sighed, after one reviewer dubbed his essay "charming and perverse." His ideas appeared wildly out of tune with the times, and the little book did not make his name or fortune.

Luminaries like Baudelaire apart, his contemporaries did not know what to make of it.

The qualities which made his essay hard to stomach in mid-nineteenth-century France are the ones that make it so arresting today. *Du Dandysme et de George Brummell* is a morally disconcerting work that retains the ability to shock. Barbey glories in turning conventional categories on their heads. Vanity? "Let us learn to say this word without horror... It is a universe less narrow than love." Extravagance? "A word used by moralists in the way that "nerves" are used by doctors" (i.e. as a convenient explanation for every ill). Caprice? "Even caprice has its codes, its inflexible laws." Frivolity? "A hateful name given to a series of what at base are entirely legitimate preoccupations, since they correspond to real needs ... To the dullards of grave morality, the glory of frivolity was an insult."

The strangest thing about Barbey's apotheosis of dandyism is not that it should have come from a Frenchman — elegance and frivolity are things we automatically associate with France — but that his hero should have been an Englishman. Surely there was no lack of French men of fashion the author could have taken as his model? Barbey pre-empts the objection. France had its exquisites too, but none of them were on his idol's level. Magnificos such as Richelieu (the eighteenth-century libertine, not the Cardinal) and the nineteenth-century Count d'Orsay had their dandified aspects, but for them the cultivation of elegance and manners, unlike for Brummell, was not their sole function in life. And Barbey has a typically perverse explanation for why only England could have given the world Beau Brummell.

The English are described as "Northern, lymphatic, pale, cold as the sea of whom they are the sons ..." Yet Brummell was the natural product of his race, since in the very austerity of his devotion to style there was a hint of Puritanism. Brummell's idea of sartorial elegance, never showy, became increasingly conservative and restrained. Byron said that there was "a certain exquisite propriety" in his clothes. The Rev. George Crabbe thought him so refined he did not regard him as a dandy at all. And Max Beerbohm later wrote of "the utter simplicity of his attire" and "his fine scorn for accessories".

Yet that does not answer the question of how the cold, lymphatic English came to produce highly original figures. Barbey's response was the claim that societies that groan under the tedium of convention "erupt in caprice", and the great dandy emerged in a country that was terminally bored with its own hypocrisy. Traders and moneymen they may have been, but that was exactly why "The English are greedier for emotions than for guineas". Crushed beneath the yoke of custom and domestic virtue, infected and re-infected with the "germs of Puritanism", they yearn to escape from themselves. This was why dandyism, in its pure state, took root on the English side of the Channel.

These are persuasive points, but we are at liberty, from our later perspective, to add our own reasons. One is perhaps that, in fashion as in politics, the English are adept at making rules and then breaking them in such a way that both the rules and the rule-makers remain the same as before. George Orwell wrote of an Etonian friend turned Marxist who nevertheless kept the bottom of his waistcoat unbuttoned, in the fashion laid down by Edward VII; his point was that we were never in much danger of revolution from such people. It is a commonplace that the English are also experts at role playing and character acting, and Brummell, like many of his descendants, was nothing if not a poseur. And of course English sensitivities are acutely alive to anything to do with social nuance, whether accent, posture, conduct or clothes. Combined with our talent for the useful in the arts rather than the abstract or sublime (Max Beerbohm called dandyism one of the decorative arts) this helps to explain our pre-eminence in tailoring. Charles Frederick Worth dictated fashion in France a century and a half before Galliano, and Fred Astaire wore Savile Row suits.

On the social significance of dandyism Barbey's message is interestingly uncertain, productively confused. He admires the high society that gave us Brummell, but does not portray dandies as the *fine fleur* of the aristocracy. What seems to have most attracted him to his hero, and what gives his essay its deeper interest, was the dandy's stance of indolent superiority not just over the masses, but over all comers. The dandy of dandies was not only above the aristocracy, the bourgeoisie and the herd: he saw himself as above royalty too. Nobody was beyond the reach of his impertinence, and no one but Brummell would have dared to say "Who's your fat friend?"

in the hearing of the Prince, justly sensitive about his ponderous mind and ugly bulk. For the same reason Barbey admired the French dandy Lauzun, a commoner who famously said to his wife, a cousin of Louis XIV, "Henrietta de Bourbon, take off these boots for me."

Brummell had moved in the highest circles of his day, and had always been a snob in the classic sense — a boy at a public school who was *sine nobilitate* and who consequently put on a show. Yet he was not a cheap or stupid snob: the man who in some respects aped the aristocracy was also keen to show himself more than their match, as he certainly was in matters of taste. So it is that Brummell the snob and social climber can also be classified historically as a bourgeois individualist, who grew up when the French revolution was having its effects in Britain, and whose reaction against the old aristocracy took the form of simplifying and refining its extravagant clothes and boorish manners. In Brummell's reign silks, velvet and jewels for men were out. And for what it is worth, while devoid of political interests or convictions, Brummell affected Whig sympathies.

The fact that he was a bit of an upstart, a man who lived literally off his wits, helps to explain both the length of his exile and the depth of his poverty. Though some of his aristocratic friends sent him gifts to keep body and soul together, and passed round the hat when he was jailed for debt, they did not exert themselves to the point of bailing him out, as they might have done for one of their number. That is why Brummell languished for nearly half his life abroad. Even in his heyday he had to content himself with appearing at the top of the non-noble guest lists in the press. For all his aristocratic affectations and associations, in the end he was not one of them.

This is not to say that he entertained any sympathy for the common man. His contempt for ordinary people was one of the least endearing aspects of an often unattractive character. And it was not affected. When he was thrust up against them in exile, where his reduced circumstances forced him to associate with English businessmen, drifters, and debtors like himself, his horror of them grew. If he could not associate with well-born folk, he preferred the company of dogs and cats. When sent to prison in Caen he was indignant beyond words: "Imagine a position more wretched than mine. They have put me in with the common people." He had a way of gaining their affection when they were useful to him, but in jail his closest companion turned out to be a former butler. His experiences there most certainly did not inspire any interest in prison reform.

Towards the end, when his mind was going and he gave up any pretence of consideration for those he saw as beneath him, his behaviour became both petty and contemptible. The best instance was when, in Caen, he sent some paté he had ordered from Paris to a *bon bourgeois* in the hope of being included in a dinner. Duly invited, he was appalled when the paté was not served. Discovering via his servant that it was being kept for a family event, and horrified at the waste, he ordered him to purloin it from the kitchen, and took it home.

In Barbey's eyes Brummell was a free spirit; a man who was on the inside of society yet at the same time playing games with it. Though he sometimes appeared to see them as belonging together, in the end Barbey was more concerned with style than with breeding. For him the "majesty" of Brummell's caprice set him above class, and made him a man apart. He himself could be a shameless snob, and dandified aristocrats like Byron figure high amongst his idols. But then so does Sheridan, a commoner yet "the font of every virtue." In his romantic imagination he appears to have seen dandies as a brotherhood of higher types. A sort of meritocracy of style and sardonic intelligence, they were the true princes of the world.

So it is pointless to seek to explain Brummell simply as a social climber attempting to equal or surpass his betters purely by his manner or attire. To Barbey he was something more elevated and more profound: the epitome of English orginality. And the Frenchman was careful to draw a distinction between originality and mere eccentricity, for which he had no time: "That way madness lies." For him Brummell was an original in the highest sense, not a clownish eccentric in the mould of Sir Lumley Skiffington, a contemporary who painted his face and wore coloured, satin suits.

Of course Brummell's behaviour was a mass of affectations, but how else, Barbey remarks with brutal realism, was he to establish his command over a highly affected society? And along with his perfectly judged manners (not the same as perfect manners, since his perfection was calculated to boost his vanity by putting others down) Brummell had genuine taste; his outfits were never contrived to draw attention to himself by crude external show. Not for him the frills or perfume for men that were then in fashion. An ascetic of the exquisite, he maintained a detached irony that was as studied and refined as his gloves or pantaloons.

But as Barbey never tires of insisting, when it comes to the definition of the true dandy, clothes were less than the half of it; it was the carefully calibrated provocation of his personal style that endeared him to the author. "It takes so much finesse to be impertinent," says the Frenchman. We must assume he knew what he was talking about.

Though highly engaging, his essay — a piece of intellectual dandyism in itself — is not always an easy read. The lengthy footnotes, though containing some of his sharpest observations, can be maddeningly digressive. And for all his exalted style, his admiration for Brummell can sound like the demented adulation of a fan for his pop idol. With its mantras of praise for the greatest dandy of them all, interspersed with brilliant perceptions couched in striking phrases, the effect is of something a precocious mind might produce on drugs.

At times he becomes lost in his own paradoxes. One minute he insists on the inimitable Englishness of dandyism. The next he suggests that its origins may have been French, and that the word itself may even have had a French etymology. (This seems doubtful: its first recorded use was as a diminutive of Andrew. Moreover the song Yankee Doodle Dandy, since appropriated by the Americans, was first sung by Englishmen mocking the appearance of American troops.)

And having claimed that dandyism was a delayed, home-grown reaction against Puritanism, he then says that a preoccupation with stylishness had entered England a century earlier at the Restoration, an import from Paris by the exiled courtiers of Charles II. Such speculations are of doubtful value; if he was going to track the more recent origins of English dandyism to their source, the Elizabethans would perhaps have made a better starting point.

His most glaring self-contradiction however goes to the heart of his thesis, and is also the most thought-provoking. This is the claim that dandyism *à la Brummell* was an historical episode, confined to one country and one era, something never to be repeated, and symbolised in a single man. Barbey's idol could exist only in a society that was "aristocratically complicated", like the England of the time, and he had no interest in the coming age of the common man, other than to deplore it. "The day that the society that produced dandyism is reformed there will be no more dandyism."

The resurgence of dandyism in our own day shows that he was spectacularly wrong on one point. Others have made the same mistake. Traditionally dandyism has been seen as lasting from Brummell to the late Victorians such as Max Beerbohm or Oscar Wilde, and as being incompatible with democracy and the mass society. "Alas!" exclaimed Baudelaire. "The rising tide of democracy that disrupts and levels everything is slowly drowning these last representatives of human pride, and with its waves of oblivion destroys the traces of these prodigious fellows."

More recently Roland Barthes added his voice to those who believe that modernity and raw consumerism had finally killed the dandy off: "reduced to a freedom to buy, dandyism could only suffocate and expire"

This seems far too restricted a view; nor does it accord with the logic of Barbey's analysis. "We shall never have a dandy like Brummell," he wrote, "but people like him, whatever weight the world gives them, we can be sure there will always be, even in England." And in the preface to the second edition he announced: "Dandyism has its roots in human nature in all countries and at all times, since vanity is universal. It is one of the thousand threads that go to make up that devilishly complex and sometimes deranged instrument, human nature. For the moment it is asleep but one day it will awake."

This makes greater sense. For if dandyism is defined as vanity, frivolity, hedonism, a preoccupation with externals and above all a posture of ironic detachment from the world, such vices (or virtues) will persist through social and political change. To that extent Barbey's essay accomplishes the exact opposite of his intention. For even as he assures us that Brummell and the values he incarnated are unrepeatable, he describes him in terms that lay bare the mainsprings of the dandyist approach to life in all times and places.

And so to the most intriguing question of all: who are the dandies of modern times? One way to find out is to test the dandyish attributes as defined by Barbey against our contemporary experience.

To begin with the externals: a dandy is most immediately recognisable by the fanatical care he or she takes with their appearance. A single example illustrates the continuity between the Age of Elegance and our own. One of the most outré devices Brummell and his circle hit upon was of distressing their clothes by rubbing the cloth with glasspaper. Barbey swoons at their daring:

"They were at the end of their impertinence, they just couldn't go any further ... They had their clothes distressed before they put them on, all over the cloth, to the point where it was no more than a sort of lace — a cloud. They wanted to walk in clouds, these gods!"

Such aristocratic caprice seems alien to our era — until we remember that before the clothes companies began to do it for them people would wash and re-wash, or fray and fret their jeans. Their aim is elegance but the form it takes has been stood on its head. When young (or middle-aged) people go to infinite pains to degrade the cloth of their denims or buy them ready-aged their intention is not to create an effect of lace, of airy aristocracy, but the opposite: to present themselves as notional members of a largely defunct industrial or agricultural manual working class. They do not want to walk as gods, but as equally mythical proletarians.

Baudelaire said that dandies were the last gasp of the aristocracy, but he also said that they were a new aristocracy in themselves. In an egalitarian society the dandyism and the vanity it implies may be inverted, but it is dandyism nonetheless. And when Barbey says that what matters are not the clothes, but how they are worn ("One can wear rumpled clothes, and still be a Dandy") he sounds like any fashion commentator you care to name.

Today there are millions "putting on the style". In dress terms the origins of the democratic dandy can be traced to before the Second World War. The "poor look" became fashionable at the time of the Depression (it recurred in 1970s Punk). Gangster chic (dark shirts with light suits and ties, with louche manners to match, in vogue again today) dates from the same period: James Cagney set the tone in *The Public Enemy* of 1931. It was not long before the French designer Paul Poiret was predicting that high fashion would one day be dominated by styles drawn from the street. Street-smartness in Britain was influenced by the more democratic United States, where the zoot suit sported by bandleader Cab Calloway became popular amongst urban blacks. (1943 saw the remarkable spectacle of the Zoot Suit Riots, sparked off by clashes between servicemen and zooties, whose dandyish nonchalance enraged the troops.)

Examples of everyday wear becoming fashion items are endless: (designer) jeans have their origin in the denims worn by American agricultural workers, chinos are so called because they were made in China for US servicemen abroad, and the shell-suit affected by the mock-black-chic comedian Ali G harks back to the single-piece suit of clothes designed by Russian and Italian futurists as the classless costume for workers of all descriptions.

In Britain the point at which dandyism began to come from below rather than above coincided neatly with the advent of the postwar socialist government. Even then the Teddy Boys of the 1950s adopted, no doubt unconsciously, aristocratic styles. Their drainpipe trousers and velvet lapels harked back to the Edwardian era, when the corpulent "Bertie" (Edward VII) and his friends were seen as men of style and leisure. (The Duke of Windsor, also seen in his time as a man of fashion, was to help popularise the wearing of sportswear.) Alan Sillitoe's *Saturday Night and Sunday Morning* reminds us that the Teddy Boys devoted an even greater proportion of their money than Brummell, if not of their time, to ensuring they had the right clobber. Mods and Rockers reflected the tensions between indigenous and Americanised dandyism in clothes and music.

Autonomy stands high in the dandy canon, but in a mass society "doing your own thing" can cause street dandyism to run riotously to seed. Eccentricity for its own sake (frowned on by Brummell and Barbey) took over from disciplined originality, and degenerated into a carnival of clothes: Afghan yaks and combat gear and army surplus and mendicant bearded Jesuses and jeans and T-shirts and granny this and that and Crombie coats and Nazi gear and beads and beads and beads. Later styles of dandyism took the more conservative form of designer clothes, but as the perennial popularity of jeans and casual styles demonstrated, the impetus still came from the bottom.

At a time when the market in nonconformity is approaching saturation, whither now the dandyish posture in clothes? If we are to believe fashion gurus such as Malcolm McLaren, who have derided the designer uniform in favour of individually tailored clothes, we may have gone full circle, and for those who can afford it a new, more directly Brummellian form of personalised dandyism could be in the wind.

Yet clothes, it can never be stressed enough, are merely the outward sign of an inward disposition. True dandyism, aristocratic or pseudo-proletarian, is a philosophy. This need not imply a highly intellectualised view of the world. Brummell was nobody's fool, though even Barbey concedes that his cleverness was not displayed in polished wit (the epigrams he bequeathed are surprisingly few) or literary ability (his letters are inflated in style, and he wrote indifferent poems). His intelligence was not conveyed through the usual channels, but by intonation, by a look, a gesture, even by silence. "This man, too superficially judged, possessed such a powerful intellect that he reigned even more by his presence than by his words."

Today we might say that, though Brummell was not the brightest and best of his generation in conventional terms, he was "a personality" who was "strong on attitude." Well before the word acquired its modern connotations his biographer, Captain Jesse, described him as "cool and impertinent". "Cool" is now a term of approval, yet it also signifies effrontery, a quality Barbey admired in Brummell above all else, even when it went along with grossly egotistical behaviour. So what? is the tenor of his response. Dandies "prefer to astonish than to please ... Dandyism is a product of a bored society, and boredom makes you bad."

There seems little need to labour the parallels with

dandyism in its modern, demotic guise. The Frenchman's words at once conjure the spectacle of celebrities who cultivate a "bad boy" or "rude girl" image. Like them Brummell was widely admired, even by those who fell reluctantly under his spell, or felt the sting of his irony, and like his the behaviour of our contemporary dandies affords pleasure, if only because it "drew society from its torpor." Brummell, in other words, had entertainment value.

As in some of Brummell's modern equivalents, alongside the studied defiance and supercilious stances there was a dry humour, and his posturing had an element of play-acting and of comic excess. Even J.B. Priestley, whose feet were closer to the ground than those of Barbey, found himself confessing that "In the days of his absurd glory, try as we might to avoid acknowledging it, there is something mysteriously impressive about Beau Brummell." If we are honest we will admit that the same is true of many of his modern-day reincarnations in the celebrity world. Mass societies can be as oppressed by feelings of *taedium vitae* and satiety as aristocracies (more, perhaps, since they are oppressed by their own weight and sameness). And however vulgar, absurd, preposterous or ludicrously affected our contemporary dandies may appear, like Brummell in his time, they answer a social need. One we are free to regret but not to deny.

"One of the dandy's main characteristics is never to do what is expected of him." For Barbey, capriciousness is a supreme virtue, and caprice is hardly in short supply in our times, albeit in what Brummell would have seen as the debased forms of novelty, the desire to shock, whimsicality and quirkiness. (He would be in a poor position to criticise: his own *mots*, characterised by a willed originality, could be somewhat laboured). And the aim of capriciousness in its modern forms is not always to charm. (The antics of the Oasis singers are an obvious example.) In fact it can frequently be to offend, for exactly the same reasons as Brummell: to exalt the dandy's vanity above the conformist mass. Dandies can be highly dislikeable people, whose affectations we love to hate, and who for that reason are in perennial demand. "He displeased too generally not to be sought after", it was said of Brummell — a remark that continues to apply to many of today's more dandified media personalities.

Another point of comparison between the age of Brummell and our own is relations between the sexes, and the dandy's attitude to women is one of the most evocative in modern terms. Brummell never took a wife, preferring the company of married society women, preferably duchesses, and best of all the Duchess of Devonshire, to that of younger women. "He had too much self-love ever to be in love," says Captain Jesse, though given his social ambitions and financial extravagance it is surprising he did not try harder to engineer a match with a suitable heiress, where love would be inessential. Noting how Brummell shies from emotional attachment, as always Barbey has an explanation: "To love, even in the least elevated sense, means to desire, which means to be dependent ... His triumphs with women were insolent because they were disinterested, and he never became giddy from the heads he turned ..."

It is to Brummell's credit that two of the women he most admired — Lady Hester Stanhope and Harriette Wilson — were women of quality, in more than the social sense. Lady Stanhope was an intelligent, truly original and unusually independent-minded woman who ended by settling in the Lebanon, where she is said to have looked like a man and to have smoked the local pipe. Of Brummell she remarked that he paid her the compliment of talking sensibly; a compliment she returned. Once she advised him to give himself fewer airs. Another time she asked why such a clever man did not devote his talents to some higher purpose. Brummell's reply — that he behaved as he did because it was the only way he could place himself in a prominent light and separate himself from the herd — was surprisingly honest.

Harriette Wilson was another highly independent woman. In her memoirs Wilson called Brummell cold, heartless and satirical, which indeed he was, but she herself was the opposite of a shrinking flower. A professional and highly successful courtesan, she attracted men less by her beauty than by her spirit and scandalous talk. She and Brummell were to some extent competitors; Barbey says of her that she was "more jealous of his reputation than of his heart." In our own day Wilson and Stanhope would be described as liberated women, and Wilson's relationship with Brummell is suggestive of a hedonistic era when competing vanities had adulterated or displaced romantic love.

It is easy to see the two of them translated to our time as a pair of celebrities more concerned with their careers than with their affections. Not surprisingly it has been suggested that the revival of dandyism and the turkey-cock male owes much to sexual rivalry, as men fail to see why women should (as it seems to them) encroach on their terrain in the professional world while retaining the monopoly of dressing up.

Historically speaking celibacy appears to have been the general rule for dandies. Emotional attachments to women compromise their autonomy, and it is certainly hard to imagine the manically fussy Brummell cohabiting with anyone, or indulging in messy, uninhibited affairs. (His one attempt at elopement had a stagey quality about it, and came to nothing.) The true dandy throws off all the constraints and duties of sex, whether of monogamy, paternity, or thraldom to the hearth. If there is an opposite of the family man, it is he. But he is not a skirt-chaser either. Brummell is portrayed by both Jesse and Barbey as sexually inert, chaste almost, at a time when licence was the norm. Again the modern echoes seem clear. In the post- as in the pre-Victorian era licence is once again the norm, and licence leads to satiety. Passion does not go with the cold languor, the eyes glazed with indifference, and the dandy's cool ("his indolence did not permit him to have verve").

Barbey suggested that English dandyism was an escape from the horrors of Puritanism. But the dandy's very fastidiousness contains one aspect at least of the Puritan disease. "What worries me about the position of the dandy and has kept me apart from them," Maurice Barrès wrote, "is the disguised Puritanism, the *noli me tangere* — you abstract yourself from life, from its stains and failures. In the end I prefer to roll in the mud with others." There was certainly something prissy about Brummell's sex-life, or lack of it; it was the only field where he failed to behave in a self-indulgent and sybaritic fashion. He was a gambler, a fastidious but hearty eater, and an occasionally heavy drinker. "In the tedium of this indolent, English existence, from which dandyism only half-escapes, he sought the feelings of that other life, a life that tingles and dazzles, that one finds in the depths of drink." Again there is little difficulty in relating this side of his personality to our own hedonistic times. In his declining years in France Brummell sometimes resorted to laudanum, to dull pain or to relieve boredom. The one thing we can be sure of is that, today, he would be a recreational consumer of cocaine (Ecstasy would be too vulgar).

Our instinctive association of fashion with camp, and Brummell's somewhat dispassionate relations with women, will inevitably raise suspicions that he was gay. There appears no evidence for this. Quentin Crisp has remarked how the mannerisms of camp appear to be perennial, and as far as we can judge there was nothing camp about the Beau, in the sense of being flaunting or excessive: as noted his style, manners and dress were in many ways austere. It is easier to see him as sexless, sufficient to himself, like those super models who have reached such a pitch of sophistication they become a strangely un-erotic presence.

Dandyism in its essence is not a homosexual condition. The confusion however is natural. Homosexuals can be and frequently are dandies, but their sexuality is an adjunct, rather than at the centre, of the dandy's creed. The estrangement of the thorough-going dandy is not from women, but from life. At its inception as a conscious movement dandies, real or aspirant, do not appear to have been predominently gay: Baudelaire and Barbey himself, hyper-active heterosexuals, are obvious examples. It was only towards the end of the nineteenth century, at the time of the fin de siècle aestheticism of Wilde and Robert de Montesquiou, and the decadence of Huysmans, that dandyism and homosexuality became more or less synonymous, and that one was taken for the outer garb of the other. Since then the most celebrated dandies — Proust, Noel Coward, Harold Acton, and Neil "Bunny" Roger — have been gay.

Nevertheless Brummell's self-infatuation evokes an impression of what used to be called inversion, a view of him that Barbey inadvertently encourages when he speaks of "Double and multiple natures ... androgynes of history ...", and suggests on several occasions that there is something feminine in the dandy which goes beyond a preoccupation with appearance. Though of course it includes that too: "For Dandies as for women to appear is to be." Naturally this aspect of Brummell has attracted the attention of feminists, who see the dandy as breaking down sexual stereotypes and the repression they can involve. To the extent that there was an androgynous element in Brummell, it is one that is echoed in many a modern dandy, whether pop stars, celebrities, or more obviously leading lights in the fashion trade. It may be too much to say that camp is what dandyism has become in a mass culture, but one could be forgiven for believing it.

All this raises the question: why is it that dandyism has been largely confined to men? Amongst the more obvious reasons is that a meticulous regard to dress has never been thought unusual in women. A deeper though equally simple reason has to do with the traditional social, political, sexual and economic dominance of the male. To be a dandy was to put oneself above society, and in the conditions of the time this would not have been a credible stance for women. Key attributes of dandyism — the detachment, the irony, the impertinence, the nihilism, the provocation — depended on an underlying autonomy women have rarely enjoyed. Now that women are winning more power and independence we shall no doubt see more female dandies.

The lines of continuity between the classical and modern dandy seem clear, and the portrait of the democratic dandy comes into focus. He or she would be a stylish creature, ultra-conscious of clothes, elegantly rather than outrageously dressed. They would be sex symbols of some kind, though in a distant and ambiguous way. They would be "smart" rather than intellectual, at once laid-back yet hedonistically engaged with life. And their vanity and detachment would entail a relentlessly sardonic view of the world. The modern dandy would be someone who had taken up an ironic posture towards society and was living it out in scrupulous detail. And most important of all, in a populist age the dandy would not ape upper class manners or dress; on the contrary, in clothes, manner and opinions they would be ultra-democratic.

For obvious reasons modern dandies are less likely to form exclusive social cliques. In a mass age we must expect our dandies to be mass-produced. Dandyism has also acquired an international dimension, and a key to an understanding of the democratic dandy is Andy Warhol. His genius consisted of glorifying the ordinary, of making celebrities of the people, of dandifying the mass. Today this means giving mass man what he most needs and desires: an illusion of individuation. In the last resort it is of course a sleight of hand. Yet insofar as it is all a sophisticated joke it is one that responds to the needs of modern society, just as Brummell's affectations responded to the highly affected society of his time.

The similarity between Warhol and Brummell runs through everything from their self-conscious appearance and meticulously planned "happenings" (social encounters in Brummell's case) to the studious manufacture of a counter-cultural persona. The hedonism, the androgyny, the irony, the "cool", the stylish vacuity — everything is there. Both cultivated a laconic verbal manner, and in each case their influence and authority rested, as Barbey remarks of Brummell, "more on presence than on words." The age in which they lived and their social status were clearly different (though as it happens Warhol rose to fame from a comfortable middle-class background), but historical circumstance is of limited importance. The point is not to contrast aristocratic with democratic dandies, but to trace the continuity of human traits; vanity and a sense of style transcend economic or social orders. Brummell had his pantaloons distressed, Warhol made a fetish of worn jeans. He would love to have invented them, he said, for had he done so, that would have been "something to be remembered by, something mass."

One was setting the tone for a few thousand members of high society, the other for millions; Brummell was a purveyor of dandyism to His Majesty the Prince Regent, Warhol sold factory-produced silk-screen prints of Marilyn Monroe as art for the crowd. One glamorised the individual, the other the multitude, exploiting their yearning for stylishness in an age of mass consumerism by referring them back to themselves. For "the masses" are ultimately individual men and women, which is to say people who can be as much slaves to elegance — or to self-image and to self-indulgence — as Brummell.

If dandyism is seen as an attitude of mind more than a mere code of dress, the difference between the two men becomes merely social and numerical. They played to different audiences, one larger than the other, but Warhol and Brummell would have instantly realised what the other was about, and their shared philosophy rested on a similar kind of nihilistic playfulness. In response to Lady Hester Stanhope's rebuke about the fatuity of his behaviour Brummell said, "If the world is so silly as to admire my absurdities, you and I may know better, but what does it signify?" The observation is easy to imagine in Warhol's mouth.

The consumer imperative ensures that today's styles

change with dizzying speed, with a constant search for the novel and outrageous ("They were at the end of their impertinence, they just couldn't go any further ..." writes Barbey), and our mass-market Brummells can have a hard time keeping up. No sooner do popular idols set a fashion than it is snatched from them by a million hands, and needs to be reinvented. That too has its dandyist rationale: ephemerality and living for the moment are as central to Brummell's concept of the dandy as they were to Warhol's idea of each of us being famous for fifteen minutes.

In a mass age the true original is the man who looks and behaves today in the way that everyone will look and behave tomorrow. The day after that a new style will be decreed, and consumers will fall into line. What does it matter? In the dandyist philosophy impermanence alone endures.

Other than Warhol himself, who are our demotic dandies? What used to be an attitude of mind confined to aesthetes, decadents or a leisured class of fashionables today enfolds large swathes of society. Candidates to match the prospectus are so numerous it is hard to decide where to start. Once you begin thinking in Brummellian terms you find yourself surrounded, in films, literature or life, by dandy or would-be dandy types. The Mafia hero in *The Godfather*. Robert de Niro in *Casino* or John Malkovich launching his own fashion collection. And in literature, the stylish cool-hearted prose of authors like Nabokov or his disciple Martin Amis.

On a mundane level it is the chat show host with his (more or less) elegant sarcasms, his impudent talk, his stylish gear (and in the case of Jonathan Ross, his Wildean mane). The "It" girl who does nothing but be herself thrives in a society so style-conscious it no longer bothers to ask what "it" signifies; all we need to know is that it is the opposite of "naff". The style journalist with his or her modish nihilism and demotic postures ("nah," "natch"), coupled with an infinite knowingness about brand names, celebrities, fame of every sort (the inverted equivalent of Brummell's name-dropping). This whole nexus of modern dandyish attitudes — smart talk, glamour, posturing, cool — was neatly summed up in a sequence at the hairdressers' in Bret Easton Ellis's satire on fashion, *Glamorama*:

"I want sideburns" Bingo moans. "I need elongation."

"Forget about natural", Didier says. "Just go for the edge."

"Doesn't anyone shampoo anymore?" Velveteen shudders. "My God."

"I want a rough style, Bingo. I want a bit of meanness. A hidden anger. There has to be a hidden anger. I want the aggressive side of this boy."

"Aggressive? He's a pastry chef at Dean and Delucca."

"I want the aggressive pastry chef look."

"Didier, this boy is about as aggressive as a baby manatee."

"Oh God, Bingo, you're such a fussbudget" Velveteen sighs."

"Am I being challenged?" Didier asks, pacing. "I think not because I'm getting bored very quickly."

The entire conversation could be transposed, with suitable adjustments, into a scene at the toilette of a late eighteenth-century beau.

Then there is the foodie dandy, who elevates gastronomy from taste into art, luxuriating in his esoteric refinements and exotic vocabulary. Or more obviously the couturier, with his never-ending search for new ways to provoke a jaded public. (The idea that John Galliano, Alexander McQueen, Stella McCarthy and English-trained Julian McDonald should excel on the Paris fashion scene is seen as a wonder of our times. Brummell and Barbey might have winced at the flamboyant styles, but the success of the English would not have surprised the latter: "So it was that Frivolity could show its head amongst a people with strict codes of behaviour and crude militaristic tendencies, as Imagination demanded its rights in the face of a morality too prescriptive to be true.")

Or there is the dandy as controversialist, whose interest in social or political questions and concern for the welfare of humanity are as burning as Brummell's, but whose vanity is satisfied by provoking the indignation of gullible souls by affecting a sub-Wildean inversion, a teasing or quirkily non-conformist line on every question. Convictions and consistency are for dullards, whose earnestness — the worst crime in the dandy's book — is there to be mocked. Essentially this is one-upmanship, a very English game, for which there is no exact equivalent in other countries. Were Brummell alive today it is easy to imagine him writing a languorously "controversial column."

Or there is the contemporary British artist, who exhibits his or her persona as proudly as their works ("His art was his life itself", says Barbey of Brummell — a less aching banality then than it became later), and who "prefer to astonish rather than to please." There is as little point in criticising Tracey Emin for her lack of meaning as there is in accusing Brummell of fatuity. For is not the dandy (in the words of Joseph Lemaitre) both revolutionary and illusionist, who "makes you believe in something that does not exist"? Seen this way Gilbert and George, for example, are also art dandies rather than the iconoclasts they appear to believe themselves to be.

Most obvious of all these real or would-be modern-day Brummells is the languid pop star (Jarvis Cocker rather than the Beatles). Cocker is a clever fellow, but note how easily Max Beerbohm's description of Brummell translates into modern times: "The Beau très dégagé, his head most supercilious upon its stock, one foot advanced ... the very deuce of a pose." Most pop stars too have devoted many an hour to getting themselves up in exactly the right, meticulously casual or asexual rig. They too exude a "sumptuous impudence", which does not prevent them being worshipped by their mass audience, in the way that Brummell was the idol of his caste. They too are frequently persons of cultivated nonchalance who look out at the world, emptily ironic, from their record sleeves, their concert posters, or the pages of the press. And when enough records have been sold, and their fortunes made, they will be pictured alongside their Rolls on the drive of their country residence — a house that may even have belonged, in Regency times, to a Beau of

Brummell's acquaintance. And just as Brummell associated with Royalty, they will be happy to perform in Pop at the Palace for the Royal Jubilee.

All these figures are dandies of our age, exquisites of postmodernity suitably packaged and popularised for democratic times. And in our day of mass-production, when the media magnify trends and dictate taste, dandaical styles and attitudes are not confined to celebrities, but are instantly mimicked by the millions they play to. (Though we must be careful not to cast the net too wide. David Beckham enjoys dressing up, but this family man and team-player is too straightforward a fellow to be a dandy in the true sense. Nor is Elton John, whose addiction to dressing up is too extravagant.)

The pop star's politics may frequently be socialistic and egalitarian, if not stagily revolutionary. Yet the whole point of Barbey's thesis is that dandies as a type are not what they seem, and it is important to look beneath the postures. The dandy's relation to power and authority, in Brummell's time as today, is deeply ambiguous. Barbey and Baudelaire saw dandyism as resulting from social disjuncture and decline, "the last spark of heroism amidst decadence", at a time when the aristocracy was losing its powers and allure and the bourgeoisie was on the rise. Both Brummell and his modern equivalents present themselves as outsiders, aloof, superior, a living provocation. The only difference between them is that one provokes from above, the other from below.

The "rebels" of both eras make their careers in the system, be it aristocratic or democratic, and it would be a mistake to take their impertinences too seriously. For in terms of their impact on the social and economic order, that is all the pop singer's radical lyrics or the artist's "subversive" exhibits frequently amount to: impertinences. The same was true of Brummell. His public insult to the Prince Regent did not mean that he had turned republican, any more than the pop star's anti-Establishment stance means that he or she is in any hurry to overturn the system in which they have made their millions and their fame. As Cyril Connolly noted in his essay *Anatomy of Dandyism:* "Dandyism is capitalist, for the Dandy surrounds himself with beautiful things and decorative people and remains deaf to the call of social justice. As a wit he makes fun of seriousness, as a lyricist he exists to celebrate things as they are, not to change them." Even when he makes a show of poking the Establishment in the eye, Connolly might have added. For beneath the (now rather dated) radical affectations the reality is that politics is seriously out of fashion.

Both Brummell and the pop star are reacting against (or exploiting) what Barbey sees as a recurring strain of Puritanism, ennui and spleen in English life. And both depend on these conditions to create their effects. So it is that they play the role of outsiders and insiders simultaneously: "Dandyism ... plays games with the rules while continuing to respect them. It suffers from their constricting effects and takes its revenge, tolerating them all the while. It invokes them even as it breaks free from them. It governs them and is governed by them in its turn."

At the centre of their preoccupations remains personal pride, or ego-tripping as we now say. What matters to today's dandy is "attitude", "life-style", iconic status, and a platform from which he or she can flaunt their persona, their detachment, their notional insurrection against a society in which they are seen (and see themselves) as glittering adornments. And invariably the bored society is half affronted, half admiring. Like Brummell the style guru or pop star has become a social catch, whose company and good opinion are sought by the panjandrums of the day: celebrity hostesses, style magazines, Prime Ministers or princes and princesses. Princesses especially.

At the turn of the twentieth century, as at the beginning of the nineteenth, what begins as anti-convention has a way of becoming accepted as the norm. Brummell's black and white dress code, refined to the point of austerity, evolved over time into the dinner jacket, symbol of rectitude and decorum in the Victorian upper middle classes. In a similar way, casual dress has become *de rigueur* amongst our icons of the democratic order. The modern dandy may not starch his cravat, but when tie-dye was in fashion his shirts would be more exquisitely tied and dyed than anyone else's, his grunge outfits will be more painstakingly fabricated than those of lesser mortals, and to the inexpert eye his designer jeans or trainers will be distinguishable from those of others only by their price. Like his patrician forebears the egalitarian dandy will go to any lengths to exalt himself above his peers.

True, Brummell aimed to construct a unique style of perfection, namely himself, whereas the icons of today will affect fashions and postures that are infinitely reproducible, indeed seem purposely designed for imitation. Brummell was an "original" in an exclusive society, while the celebrity's dress code and persona are semi-commercial commodities, devised to be reduplicated in the clubs, bars and shopping malls of half the planet. We see about us every day of the week people who, on however humble a level, have erected stylishness and "attitude" into a philosophy. Like Brummell they are possessed by self-image, even if the image is collective, an off-the-peg assemblage of name-tags and musical preferences and football teams.

How has this inversion come about? Prosperity, as well as democracy, is a key. An age of elegance, aristocratic or demotic, presupposes a high degree of stability and wealth. The Regency coincided with an upsurge in prosperity which made possible a period of self-indulgence amongst the upper classes, where in the words of the historian Arthur Bryant "the rich had become almost too rich for reason." Our own obsession with style and fashion is also developing in an age of unprecedented leisure, which now extends through much of society, and an aspiration towards elegance, if not elegance itself, has come within the reach of millions. Provided we are prepared to devote enough time to it, for relatively little money, we can all be dandies now — albeit of the reduplicated, Warholian variety.

The lad about town who spends everything that remains after he has satisfied his drink or drug habit on his gear, and who cultivates an ever-modish contempt towards "conventional" society, inhabits the same universe as Brummell (and in financial terms may well suffer a not dissimilar fate). The office worker who overdraws her account to ensure she has exactly the right shoes, eye-shadow and the rest, and whose life-purpose is fulfilled when she is filmed for a few seconds on a TV show featuring girls clubbing, is the great dandy's spiritual daughter. Few can afford to have four footmen blowing perfumed powder into their locks like the Prince of Kaunitz (though the scene calls to mind film images of Madonna at her toilet, surrounded by flunkeys), but many will strain their finances to the limit to re-model their hair endlessly, or finesse it into dread-locks.

Does the democratisation of dandyism imperil taste — Brummell's god of gods? Are there in fact two forms of dandyism, one vulgar, the other exquisite? By no means all contemporary fashions are ugly or excessive, and mass taste is not invariably unrefined. In the eighteenth century elegance began and ended with Brummell and his circle; in the twenty-first it is fostered and propagated by publicly financed schools of design where fashion is cultivated for and by the people. Commercialism and consumerism can debase taste and banish discrimination; they can also be a means of spreading elegant fashions faster. Though he would be horrified to hear it said, Barbey himself was an unconscious advocate of democratic elegance: "Why should the notion of beauty not be realised in little things and elevated, thanks to grace, above mere prettiness?" No doubt he would have abhorred the charivari of ever-changing styles, and I do not see him replacing his scarlet cape and Spanish hat for combat trousers and trainers, be they never so exquisite and expensive. My hunch is that the fogeyish Frenchman would have preferred to mimic antique dandy styles.

In the case of Brummell, whose taste was better than his betters', and who had an eye for simplicity, it is impossible to be sure. Our parvenu might have been quick to see where power lay in a mass society. The self-invented fashion guru would most certainly have cultivated the celebrities of the moment, and gravitated smartly towards Diana, "the people's Princess", as swiftly as he did towards the Prince Regent. He might even have had his own fashion house, providing someone else took care of the accounts, whose absolutely inimitable and soon to be imitated styles, complete with pirated designer labels, would have conquered the world.

In his time Brummell shared the contemptuous attitude to commerce characteristic of his class, and his debtors — mere accessories to his genius — were lucky if they were paid. (A creditor, foolish enough to ask for his money, was told he had already been paid in kind. "When I was at the window of White's and you were passing, I said 'Jimmy, how are you?'"). But men of fashion are expert in sniffing the wind, and in the hyper-commercialised world of today it is not difficult to see Brummell making a sumptuous career for himself as a style guru of the kind who can be seen consorting with royalty on the pages of *Hello!* magazine.

Vanity, vanity... Should we be disapproving of the dandy's disengagement, his nihilistic stance? Not at all, says Barbey: contempt for the world is, after all, a Christian notion.

The inversion is typically deft, but its cleverness should not obscure the originality of the remark and Barbey's extraordinary anticipation of modern moods. "Futile sovereign of a futile world!" he calls Brummell. The same self-cancelling characterisation could stand as a caption on the photograph of many a sulky rock star, TV personality, haughty fashion model or billionaire style guru today.

Though remember the great Beau's appalling fate. For those of a judgemental turn of mind Barbey's essay can be read less as a celebration of the eternal dandy than as a morality tale. For did not Brummell end his days in imbecility tempered by self-delusion, and did not the progression of his madness follow the pattern of his life? The dandy, a creature of contradictions, can be fragile under stress: when he had gambled himself into bankruptcy and the exile from fashionable London it entailed, under the pressure of reality the construct Brummell had so painstakingly invented fell apart. In Caen his personality disintegrated in perfect symmetry with his fortune and his fame. Today he might have ended it all with an overdose.

Put that way the life of George Bryan Brummell becomes little more than a true-life version of the Rake's Progress. But what the industrious, finger-wagging Captain Jesse dwelt on at length Barbey skates over. The long decline and painful fall of his idol are relegated literally to a footnote, and his observations are confined to a few evasive lines. "Dandyism is stronger than reason," Barbey opines on his hero's slide into indigence and madness, and that, pretty much, is that. For us it is not so easy to brush aside the squalor of Brummell's final days. Even if we do not think in terms of retribution, it is hard not to link cause and effect. In a sense it was inevitable that Brummell should have died in such degradation. For if he was indeed the incarnation of vanity, it follows that, stripped of his self-image, Brummell was nothing.

Does the re-emergence of dandyism in an egalitarian society signal the decadence of democracy, as Brummell's was said to of the aristocracy? One hesitates to judge, still less moralise. If our theoretician of dandyism was right, and vanity rules the world, then, now and forever, much good will moralising do us. And how can you thunder against people whose very point is that they are ephemeral? Barbey has a phrase for those who sermonised against Brummell and his kind: "They are people who think they are serious simply because they don't know how to smile."

ON DANDYISM AND GEORGE BRUMMELL

JULES BARBEY D'AUREVILLY

Translator's Note

If the style of Barbey's essay was judged too precious and "over-licked" in mid-nineteenth-century France, how much more so today? The problem of rendering it into modern English is obvious. Take the first sentence: "*Les sentiments ont leur destinée.*" It is as linguistically straightforward as it is maddeningly elliptical. No translation can render it adequately because it is not something any solid, earth-creeping Englishman would dream of saying, for fear of featuring in Pseud's Corner. I am conscious that in deciding to render it baldly as "Feelings have their fate" I may be accused of writing nonsense. Yet to seek a more down-to-earth English phrase, so as to blow off the froth, would risk rendering a would-be grandiloquent phrase too literal-mindedly. It would also lose the almost bravura Frenchness of Barbey's style — a dandy style if ever there was one, perfectly suited to its subject.

The French text is full of such exasperating phrases. In excessively obscure places I have relaxed my guiding rule, which is not to be too afraid of the English sounding French. In such cases, for purposes of clarity, I have interpreted the idea rather than the words.

A translation done in 1897 was reprinted some time ago in America, together with a brief preface by Quentin Crisp. He pronounced this now somewhat antique rendering "truly graceful, yet free of the over-elaborate, almost euphuistic style of its hero's [i.e. Brummell's] letters." Which rather dodges the issue of faithfulness to the text, but never mind. Crisp went on to confess, in fine throwaway fashion, that "on Mr d'Aurevilly's text I can express no opinion as I understand not one word of French." Perhaps this was just as well, since the translator, Douglas Ainslie, got over the problem of Barbey's more over-cooked and intractable passages by simply leaving them out in his English version.

Many styles of translation would be possible. Given the special nature of the subject, my aim has been to make Barbey's work readable in English while preserving its French flavour.

George Walden

DEDICATION

Letter to Monsieur César Daly
Director of the Review of Architecture

While you are travelling, my dear Daly, and none of the friends who think of you know where you can be found, here is something I dare not call a book, which will await you on your doorstep. It is the statuette of a man who does not deserve to be represented other than as a statuette: a curiosity of manners and of history, who merits a place in your bookshelf and your study.

Brummell is not a part of the political history of England, but he approaches it through the friendships he made in it. He has his place in a kind of history that is more elevated, more generalised, and more difficult to write — the history of English manners — for political history does not contain all social tendencies, and all are worthy of study. Brummell was the expression of one such tendency: if it were not so, his influence would be impossible to explain. To describe, to fathom this influence, and to show that it was more than superficial, could form the subject of a book that Beyle [Stendhal] has forgotten to write, and would have tempted Montesquieu.

Sadly I am neither Montesquieu nor Beyle, neither eagle nor lynx, but I have tried to see clearly into a subject which many people no doubt would disdain to explain. I offer the result to you, my dear Daly, as a man who feels grace as a woman or an artist feels it, also as a thinker who will agree it has a place in the world. It gives me pleasure to dedicate to you this study of a man whose celebrity was due to his elegance. Had it been a study of a man whose celebrity was due to his intelligence, I might justly have dedicated it to you as well, who are so richly endowed in this regard.

So pray accept this gift as a token of friendship and as a remembrance of days, happier than at present, when I saw you more often.

Yours truly,
J.A. Barbey d'Aurevilly
Passy, 19 September, 1844

So, my friend, I won't change a single word of this seventeen-year-old dedication today, and it must be the first time that seventeen years haven't changed anything. Let it remain as whole as the friendship of which it is the expression, and which has been unchanging between us, cloudless and without lapses. I have not always been as happy as I have with you, the column still standing amongst my ruins! Seventeen years! You know how that miserable Tacitus — always intolerable because he is always right — calls this passing of days, which perhaps I should have shut up about, if, in the sad business of living, I had not had at least the pleasure, my dear Daly, of being able to say that I remain for you exactly what I was so many years ago, and since everything in this book is fatuous, of using it to boast about my immortal sentiments!

J.A. Barbey d'Aurevilly
Paris 29 September 1861

I

Feelings have their fate, and there is one for which no one is prepared to show pity: vanity. Yet even as moralists deplore it in their books they show how large a place it holds in our hearts. Worldly-wise people — moralists too in their way, since they are called upon to pass judgement on life twenty times a day — uphold the verdict of the books. To listen to them you would think that vanity is the basest feeling of all.

Just as men can be oppressed, so can things. Can it be true that vanity is at the very bottom of the hierarchy of human feelings? And if it is, and has been accorded the place it deserves, why do we despise it so? Is it really the most base? The value of human feelings is surely determined by their social importance, and what could be of greater benefit to society in the hierarchy of these feelings than the restless search for the approval of others, the unquenchable thirst for applause from the gallery? In great things this thirst goes by the name of "the love of glory", in small ones, "vanity". Are love, friendship or pride so very superior to it? Love, with its thousand shades and secondary characteristics, friendship and pride are all based on a preference for another, for several others, or for oneself, and this preference is exclusive.

Vanity, on the other hand, pays attention to everything. If it sometimes displays a preference for the approval of some people rather than others, its code of honour makes it vulnerable to a single rebuttal, and vanity suffers deeply when the rose of approval is withheld. Love says to the beloved, "You are my universe". Friendship says "You are all I ask", and often, "You are my consolation." Pride, on the other hand, is silent. As a brilliant man once put it, "Pride is a solitary, indolent and sightless king, whose crown obscures his eyes." Vanity inhabits a less restricted universe than love, and what is enough for friendship does not suffice for it. It is a queen just as much as pride is a king, but it is a busy, clear-sighted queen who is widely courted, and whose crown is placed where it is most becoming.

All this needed to be said before we speak of Dandyism, that child of vanity whose father has been too often vilified, and of the Dandy George Brummell, the vainest of them all.

II

When vanity is satisfied and shows it, it becomes little more than fatuousness. That is the rather impertinent term that hypocrites of modesty (in other words, all of us) have invented because they recoil before true feeling. It would be wrong to believe, as people often seem to, that fatuous behaviour is simply the kind of vanity that men exhibit in their relations with women. No, people indulge in such behaviour for all kinds of reasons — because of their birth, wealth, ambition, or knowledge (Tufière is one example, Turcaret another). However, since we French are so preoccupied with women, we have tended to apply the word fatuous to the vanity of those who are a success with them and who think themselves irresistible.

Yet this form of fatuity is common to all cultures where women are prized. It is not to be confused with the other variety, that goes by the name of Dandyism, and which has for some time been trying to acclimatise itself in Paris. The former is vanity in its universal, human form. The latter is English vanity, which is of a particular — indeed very particular — kind. Since the language of Voltaire prides itself on having a name for everything that is human and universal, a word must be found for whatever does not, which is why the word Dandyism is not a French one.

It will remain as foreign as the thing it expresses. We can do what we can to reflect the full spectrum of its colours, but chameleons cannot reflect white, and it is in degrees of whiteness that cultures show the force of their originality. Even if we possessed the powers of assimilation that distinguish us from others in greater measure than we do, this gift of God would not supersede that other gift, that other force — the power to be oneself. It is this which constitutes the character, the very essence of a people. And it is the force of English originality when it is applied to human vanity — a vanity that is rooted deep in the heart of the lowliest kitchen-boy, and for which all Pascal's scorn was really no more than purblind insolence — that produces what we know as Dandyism.

No chance of us sharing it with England. It is as profound as her national spirit, and aping is not resemblance. You can adopt an air or strike a pose as easily as you can purloin the style of a dress coat, but in the end the game of make-believe becomes a tedious one. It is a dreadfully cruel thing to be forced to wear a mask, even for people of character who are willing to play the part of the Fieschi of Dandyism should it be necessary; how much more so for our amiable youths. The ennui they breathe and seek to inspire in others is no more than a false echo of Dandyism. They can affect their disdainful airs as much as they like, and wear their white gloves right up to the elbows, but it will not help. The land of Richelieu will never produce a Brummell.

III

These two celebrated Beaux may resemble each other in terms of the universal traits of vanity, yet they are completely different racial types, as distinct from one another as the very spirit of their respective societies. One belonged to the nervy, hot-blooded French, who allow their impulses to run to the wildest extremes. The other was descended from Norsemen. Pale and lymphatic, cold as the sea that bore them, but also as quick to anger as the oceans, they warm their chilled blood in the flames of alcohol. Yet despite their opposing temperaments both men were driven by a powerful vanity, and naturally they allowed it to shape their every action. On that score the two of them face equal censure from moralists who condemn vanity instead of analysing it, and analysis is the first step to forgiveness.

Not that we should be surprised. For eighteen hundred years the sentiment of which we speak has been repressed by the Christian notion of contempt for worldly things, an attitude that continues to dominate the least Christian of minds. Is it not the case that almost all intelligent people harbour some prejudice against their own intelligence, and do penance for it? It is this that explains the unfailingly derogatory attitude towards Brummell of those who regard themselves as highly serious people, simply because they do not know how to smile. It is what explains, better than mere party spirit, Chamfort's cruel words against Richelieu. He attacked him with a cutting, brilliant and venomous wit, as if stabbing him with a poisoned crystal dagger. In so doing Chamfort, atheist as he was, showed how much he was enslaved to the Christian ethic. Himself a vain man, he could not tolerate the idea that the sentiment from which he suffered might bring pleasure to others.

For Richelieu, like Brummell — more so even than Brummell — gloried in every sort of celebrity and satisfaction that the opinion of the world can bring. Both men succeeded by obeying the instincts of their vanity (we must learn to say the word without a shudder of horror) in the same way one obeys the instincts of one's ambition, one's love, and so on. But there the analogy ends. Not only did they have different temperaments; the contrast between them was heightened by the very different societies in which they lived. In Richelieu's case it was a society that had broken all bounds in its implacable pursuit of pleasure; Brummell's society champed at the bit of boredom. One was frankly dissolute, the other hypocritical. And it is precisely in this divergence that the difference between the fatuity of Richelieu and the Dandyism of Brummell lies.

IV

Brummell was a Dandy and nothing more. Before becoming the Beau his name now suggests, Richelieu was an imposing figure in a decaying aristocracy. He was a general in a highly militarised nation. He was handsome in an age when the senses were in revolt against the intellect and were proud to share its empire, and when the conventions of the times did not prescribe pleasure. One can conceive of another Richelieu beyond the one we know, since he had every endowment life can offer. But take away the Dandy in Brummell, and what remains? He was good for nothing more than to be a Dandy, but good for nothing less than to be the greatest Dandy, not just of his time, but of all time.

He played the part in a pure, meticulous way — innocently, one might almost say. In the rough and tumble we politely call society, fate is almost always a more powerful force than ability, or ability rises higher than fate. Yet in Brummell his nature and his destiny, his genius and his fortune, were in rare accord. Sheridan had greater wit and passion. Lord Byron was a far greater poet — for Brummell was something of a poet too. And Yarmouth was a grander noble, as was Byron. Yarmouth, Sheridan and Byron, together with many others of his era who had distinguished themselves in every field of glory, were Dandies as much as himself, but they were also something more. Brummell did not possess that distinction that in some took the form of passion or genius, in others high birth and an immense fortune. His lack of it turned out to be an advantage. Thrown back on the single force that marked him out from others he raised himself to its highest rank: he was Dandyism incarnate.

V

The trouble with Dandyism is that it is as difficult to describe as it is to define. People who see things from a narrow perspective have got it into their heads that it was above all a question of dress, of external elegance — that Dandies were merely dictators of fashion, bold and felicitous masters of the art of making one's toilet. It is most certainly that, but it is other things besides.*

Everyone gets this wrong, even the Anglo-Saxons themselves! Did not their Thomas Carlyle, author of Sartor Resartus, recently take it upon himself to speak of Dandies and Dandyism in a book he called the Philosophy of Clothes? But all he did was to sketch a picture of fashionable folk with the giddy pen of a Hogarth, then say, "There's dandyism for you!" It was not even caricature, since caricature exaggerates everything and omits nothing. Caricature is a kind of exasperation with reality, whereas the reality of Dandyism is human, social, and spiritual. A Dandy is not just a walking,

Yet it is not only by one's material aspect that one makes oneself visible. Dandyism is a whole way of being — a way of being entirely composed of nuances, as always happens in well-established and highly civilised societies, where humour becomes a rare commodity and where the force of convention scarcely has it over tedium. And nowhere has the conflict between the dictates of convention and the tedium they generate made itself felt so strongly in its habits and customs as in England, this society dominated by the Bible and the Law. And it is perhaps from this running conflict, eternal as the duel between Death and Sin in Milton, that the profound originality of this puritan society springs. In fiction it gives us Clarissa Harlowe, in reality Lady Byron.* The day that the conflict is resolved we must expect what we call Dandyism to be greatly changed, assuming it still exists at all, since it stems from this

---

*   *As writers it also gives us women such as Miss Edgeworth, Miss Aikin etc. See the memoirs of the latter on Elizabeth: the style and opinions are those of a pedant and a prude writing about a prude and a pedant.*

---

talking suit of clothes! On the contrary, what constitutes Dandyism is a particular way of wearing them. One can wear rumpled clothes and still be a Dandy. Lord Spencer managed it with an outfit that had a single coat-tail, and even that he eventually cut off, and made it into the thing that has since carried his name. At one time, believe it or not, the Dandies dreamed up a style that might be called the threadbare look. It happened under Brummell. They had reached the very limits of their impertinence, they could go no further — yet the Dandies found a way: this was the dandyish state of war between propriety and the tedium it breeds.*

It follows from all this that one of the consequences of
Dandyism, one of its principal characteristics — or rather its
character in more general terms — is always to produce the
unexpected. For this the mind that toils under the yoke of
logical rules is unprepared. Eccentricity, another fruit of the
English soil, leads to the same thing, though this time in a
blind, wild, unbridled way. Eccentricity is the rebellion of the

---

* *There is little need to insist on the boredom that gnaws at the heart
of the English, and gives them the dismal distinction of having more
suicides and more corruption than other countries devoured by this
malaise. Boredom in modern times is the child of analysis. But in the
case of the English, the wealthiest people in the world, to the boredom
that afflicts us all must be added the boredom suffered by the Romans,
which was the child of satiety. If the average modern society were
composed of sturdier souls we would have a multiplicity of Tiberiuses
in Capri — minus of course the empire.*

---

*idea (I know of no other word to express it) of having their clothes
distressed before they put them on, rubbed all over till they were no
more than a kind of lace — a mist of cloth. They were gods who
wanted to walk in their own clouds! To do it they used a piece of
sharpened glass, and the procedure was extremely delicate and time-
consuming. Now that was a true act of Dandyism. The clothes
themselves are nothing to do with it, since by that point they
scarcely existed!*

*Another example: Brummell wore gloves that moulded his hands
closely, like a wet muslin that followed the contour of his nails like
the skin itself. Yet the Dandyism did not lie in the perfection of*

individual against the established order, sometimes against nature itself, and that way madness lies.

Dandyism, on the other hand, plays games with the rules while continuing to respect them. It suffers from their constricting effects and takes its revenge, tolerating them all the while. It invokes them even as it breaks free from them. It governs them and is governed by them in its turn. A dual-natured, volatile thing, this Dandyism! To play its game you

these gloves, but in the fact that they were specially made by four craftsmen, who were artists in the matter: three for the hands and one for the thumbs.[1]

Thomas Carlyle wrote another book, On Heroes and Hero Worship. In this he gave us the Poet Hero, the Hero King, the Man of Letters as Hero, the Hero Priest, the Prophet Hero and even the God Hero. He could also have given us the Hero of Leisured Elegance — the Dandy Hero, but he forgot him. Moreover what he writes in Sartor Resartus about Dandies in general (whom he rudely describes as a 'Dandiacal sect') is more than enough to show that the muddled Germanic vision of this English Jean-Paul made it impossible for him to understand the cold and precise nuances that Brummell was all about. He would have talked about him with all the profundity of those pettifogging French historians who, in their stupidly solemn Revues, passed judgement on Brummell pretty much as some boot-maker or tailor he deigned to employ might have done. All of them are two-a-penny Dantans carving fake busts with their pocket-knives from bars of Windsor soap you would not even want in your bath!

[1] *I am so keen to be understood clearly that I will do something absurd, and insert a footnote within a footnote. Although he*

must have at your command all the suppleness that goes with elegance, in the same way that all the shades of a prism are required to form an opal.

And this was Brummell's gift. He possessed the kind of God-given elegance that is often perverted under social pressures. Still, he most certainly had it, and in exercising his gift he was responding to the needs of jaded societies, mercilessly crushed beneath the relentless rigours of propriety, for whim and caprice. He was living proof of a truth that needs to be endlessly repeated to those who live by the rules: that if you trim the wings of Fancy they will grow back even longer.*

He had that rare and charming familiarity that touches everything and profanes nothing. He lived on an equalfooting

---

* *NB The excitement Miss Essler inspired in the American press, amongst the descendants of the Puritans of old England. A case of a dancer's leg turning Roundheads!*

---

wasn't even English (he was an Austrian) the man who came closest to the English Dandies was the Prince of Kaunitz. He possessed coolness, nonchalance, a majestic frivolity and a ferocious egotism ("I have not a friend in the world!" he would declare ostentatiously). Neither the agony nor the death of Marie-Thérèse could bring forward the hour he got up or the time he devoted to his toilet, which beggared description, by a single minute. The Prince of Kaunitz was not a Dandy when he wore a satin corset like that of Alfred de Musset's Andalouse. But he was when he passed through a series of salons, whose size and number he had carefully calculated, and where valets armed with puffs powdered him as he went, simply to give the colour of his hair exactly the right shade!

with the most powerful and elevated people of his time, and by his easy manner he rose to their level. Where cleverer men than himself would have lost their footing, he stayed upright. His audacity was perfectly judged, and he could finger the axe with impunity. Some say that the blade he had escaped so many times finally cut him down, and that he made the mistake of giving the vanity of a fellow Dandy, a royal Dandy, his majesty George IV, an interest in his demise. Yet so great was his empire over them that, had he so desired, he would have reconquered it.

VI

His entire life was an influence, which is to say something that can scarcely be recounted. We are alive to an influence so long as it lasts, and when it has gone we can point to its effects. But if these effects are hard to disengage from the influence that produced them, and if they do not survive it, it becomes impossible to write their history. Herculaneum can be dug up from the ashes, but when a few years have passed the manners and customs of a society are buried more deeply than by a volcano's lava. Even memoirs, which are the history of these customs, are mere approximations.*

So we can never recover as clear and detailed a portrait as we would like of English society in Brummell's time, let alone one drawn from the life. And we will never be able to trace the

---

* *And not always even that. What use, for example, are Wraxall's Memoirs? And yet who was in a better position to observe than he?*

successive waves of influence Brummell exerted on his contemporaries to their full extent. Byron's quip — that he would rather be Brummell than the Emperor Napoleon — will always strike us as an absurd affectation, or as a piece of irony, and the true meaning of his words will tend to be lost.

Rather than showing such disrespect for the author of *Childe Harold* we should try to understand what he meant by expressing so bold a preference. As a poet and a man of imagination he was struck by the hold Brummell exercised over the imagination of a society that was both hypocritical and weary of its own hypocrisy, because he could appreciate its power. It was a vindication of the power of the individual, which appealed to his own genius more than power of any other kind.

VII

It is with words like Byron's that the story of Brummell's life will be written. And yet, as though destiny were determined to mystify us, it is those selfsame words that make the story so difficult to decipher. It is hard to justify admiration like Byron's by reference to facts which are by nature ephemeral and have perished entirely. Even the authority of the very grandest name, the tribute of the most exalted genius will only serve to thicken the mystery. The most fleeting aspect of a society is its manners. They are an aroma too subtle to be preserved and which leaves no trace, and it is this that made Brummell a prince of his time.*

Like the outstanding orator, actor, or conversationalist, like all those great minds who speak with their bodies to the

---

* *Manners are the fusion of motions of the mind and of the body, and such movements are hard to depict.*

bodies of others, as Buffon has said, Brummell is now no more than a name that emits a mysterious glow in the memoirs of the time. It is hard to explain the position he held, yet one can sense it, and it is worth trying to account for it. The present work is the first detailed study for a portrait that remains to be painted, since no one has yet shown themselves ready for the painful struggle. No thinker has so far attempted to ascertain the extent of his influence in a serious, detailed way.For Dandyism follows its law, or rather it is a deviation from the law which makes it a law unto itself. Deep minds have lacked the subtlety to do it, and subtle ones have lacked the depth.

A number have nevertheless tried their hands. Within Brummell's lifetime two well-known authors took up their pens — sharpened to exquisite points and dipped in musk-scented Chinese ink — and threw down on blue-tinted paper with silver borders a few lines where one catches a glimpse of Brummell. They were charming in the lightness of their wit and their casual perspicacity. I speak of *Pelham* and *Granby*, and of Brummell as well, to the extent that they both sought to lay down the law about Dandyism. But did they ever have the intention of portraying him, if not according to the facts of his life, then at least in the realities of his existence, with all its novelish potential? In *Pelham,* one rather doubts it. With *Granby* it is easier to believe. The portrait of Trebeck appears to have been drawn from life: those curious touches are not the kind of thing one invents, and their vividness suggests a real presence.

Yet apart from Lister's novel, where Brummell is far

more recognisable (assuming we are right to look for him there) than in Mr Bulwer's *Pelham,* there is no book in England that shows Brummell as he was, and explains the power of his character with any degree of clarity. Though recently a distinguished gentleman* has published two volumes in which he gathered together, scrupulously and with the patience of an angel, all the known facts on Brummell's life. Why is it that so much care and effort should have resulted in so diffident a chronicle, in which history reveals so few of her cards? Brummell still lacks historical explanation. He continues to have his admirers, such as the epigrammatic Cecil and inquisitive minds like that of Mr Jesse. And of course he had his enemies, though we shall name no names. Suffice it to say that among those of his contemporaries who are still with us, as among pedants of all ages — worthy folk with the intellectual equivalent of the two left feet that Rivarol accused all Englishwomen of having — there are some who feel genuinely indignant at the lustre surrounding the name of Brummell. Grave-minded moralistic blockheads like these see such frivolity as a personal insult.

The historian capable of judging the Great Dandy without partiality or hatred has yet to appear, and every day that passes makes his appearance less likely. We have explained

---

* *Captain Jesse, who has written two thick volumes on Brummell. Before publishing them he was kind enough to put at our disposal, with exemplary courtesy, the information he had on the famous Dandy.*

why. If he fails to materialise, fame will have been just another mirror for Brummell. In his lifetime, it would have reflected his image in all the glittering purity of its delicate surface. But after his death, like a mirror when there is no longer anyone left before it, it will have retained nothing of him.

VIII

Dandyism was not the invention of a single individual, but the result of a particular type of society that pre-existed Brummell. It would perhaps be appropriate to consider it in the context of the history of English culture and to establish how it came about. There is every reason to believe that its origins are French. Elegance came to England with the restoration of Charles II (who arrived arm in arm with Corruption, said at the time to be her sister and who has occasionally seemed to justify the claim) and proceeded to attack the appalling, imperturbable earnestness of Cromwellian Puritanism with the arms of ridicule and derision.

Force of habit, always deep-seated in Britain, irrespective of whether the habits be good or bad, had made things worse. To breathe freely again it was vital to escape its domination and to loosen its constricting ties. In France the courtiers of Charles II had imbibed with their champagne a lotus-eating style of life that helped them forget the sombre religious ways of their homeland and to open up a prospect of escape. A lot of people scrambled into the breach. "It was not long before the pupils had overtaken their masters, and such was their eagerness to be corrupted that the Rochesters and the Shaftsburies amongst them leapfrogged a century ahead of French morals of the time, straight into the Regency", as a writer has noted with pungent accuracy.*

We speak not of Buckingham, nor of Hamilton, nor even of Charles II, nor of all those whose memories of exile proved more powerful than their impressions on return. We have in mind those who remained English but who felt the foreign breeze at a distance, and who initiated the reign of the *Beaux*: Sir George Hevett, Wilson (said to have been killed by Law in a duel), or Fielding, whose beauty caught the sceptical eye of the feckless Charles II, and who, when married to the famous Duchess of Cleveland, played out scenes reminiscent of Lauzun with the Duchess of Montpensier.

Clearly the very name *Beaux* points to French influence, and the style of elegance they adopted reflected their name. It did not spring from native soil, did not blend with the originality of the people in whose midst Shakespeare was born, was insufficiently imbued with the deep-seated force

* *Amédée Renée, in his introduction to The Letters of Lord Chesterfield. Paris, 1842.*

that was to penetrate it later on. Let there be no mistake, the *Beaux* were not Dandies, but pre-dated them. True, Dandyism was already stirring beneath the surface, but it had not yet shown itself, and it was from the soul of English society that it would emerge. Fielding died in 1712. After him came Colonel Edgeworth, whose praises were sung by Steele (also a *Beau* in his youth) and who formed the next link in the fine-wrought gilded chain of *Beaux*. The chain ended with Nash, to be reopened with Brummell, this time with Dandyism added.

If it can be said to have been born earlier, it was in the interval that separates Fielding from Nash that Dandyism found its line of development and its form. As for its name (and again the root may well be French) it was acquired late. It is not to be found in Johnson, though the thing itself certainly existed amongst people of the highest rank, as indeed it should. Since the worth of a man is always proportionate to his faculties, and Dandyism represented precisely those faculties that were insufficiently recognised at the time, any superior man was bound to take on a dandyish aspect, and so they did. Examples include Marlborough, Chesterfield and Bolingbroke — especially Bolingbroke. Chesterfield's *Letters* were a treatise on how to be a Gentleman, just as Machiavelli had written a treatise on how to be The Prince. In them he was not so much prescribing laws as expounding the customs of his time, and he was still very much attached to conventional opinion.

As for Marlborough, though beautiful in a supercilious,

feminine way, he was more self-interested than vain. Only Bolingbroke was an advanced, all-round Dandy of those times. He alone had the boldness of conduct, the sumptuous impertinence, the preoccupation with outward effect, and the ever-present vanity. It will be recalled that, though he was jealous of Harley, who was assassinated by Guiscard, he consoled himself by saying that the assassin had doubtless mistaken one minister for another. And did he not break with the prudish ways of London salons when — horror of horrors — he displayed a love of the most natural kind for an orange-seller who kept a stall below the arcades of Parliament, and who may not even have been pretty?*

And finally, it was Bolingbroke who came up with Dandyism's motto, the *Nil mirari* of its adherents, those demigods whose aim it was always to astound whilst remaining impassive themselves.† Dandyism suited Bolingbroke better

---

* *London and Westminster Review.*

† *At the heart of the agitations of modernity Dandyism introduced an antique calm. Though whereas the calm of the ancients sprang from the harmony of their faculties and the fullness of a life freely lived, the calm of the Dandy is the repose of a mind that, though acquainted with many ideas, is too disabused to get excited. Were a Dandy to be eloquent he would speak like Pericles, with his arms crossed under his coat. See for example the exquisite, impertinent and very modern attitude of Girodet's Pyrrhus listening to Hermione's curses. That should give a better idea of what I am trying to say than anything I write here.*

than anyone else, since it betokened a freedom on questions of manners as much as in religious and moral matters. Just as philosophers erect a higher obligation before the law, so the authority of the Dandies overrode the rules that govern the most aristocratic and traditional circles.*

By their acidic wit, coupled with a softening elegance, they managed to gain acceptance for fluctuating rules of conduct which in reality were quite simply a reflection of their audacious personalities. This is a strange result, yet in keeping with the nature of things. Society may close its ranks, the aristocracy may close its mind to everything but conventional wisdom, but Caprice will invariably assert itself and break through positions that seemed impregnable, yet had long been undermined by boredom. So it was that Frivolity† could show its head amongst a people with strict codes of behaviour and crude militaristic tendencies,

---

* *And not only in England. When the Russian Princess Aschekoff failed to wear anything red it was an act of Dandyism, and possibly a dangerous one, since it proclaimed the most scandalous act of independence. In Russia red denotes beauty, and in the eighteenth century beggars on street corners would not have dared beg if they had no red about them. See Rulhière on this woman, a writer whose Dandyism lay in the flourish of his pen, and who is as piquant as he is profound. If history were no more than an anecdote, think how he would write it!*

† *The maddening name which is given to a whole series of preoccupations that are really entirely legitimate, corresponding as they do to real needs.*

as Imagination demanded its rights in the face of a morality too prescriptive to be true. Together they were translated into a science of manners and attitudes impossible elsewhere, of which Brummell was the finished expression and which will never be equalled again. We shall now see why.

IX

George Bryan Brummell was born in Westminster, the son of W. Brummell, Esquire, private secretary to Lord North. North himself was a Dandy on occasion, who, seated on his ministerial bench, slept through the most virulent opposition attacks from sheer disdain. It was he who made the fortune of W. Brummell, a man of great order and energy. Pamphleteers who cried corruption in the hope of being corrupted themselves used to call Lord North the god of emoluments, yet in paying Brummell he was doing no more than rewarding his services.

When the ministry of his benefactor fell, Mr Brummell became high sheriff of Berkshire. He lived near Donnington Castle, famous as Chaucer's birthplace, and there he exercised that lavish hospitality for which the English, alone in the world, have the feeling and the capacity. He had kept up his grand connections and frequently entertained Fox and Sheridan, amongst other contemporary celebrities. So it was

GEORGE BRUMMELL
Insolent, cynical, excellent taste
— and just a little famous.
The essence of dandydom.

JULES BARBEY D'AUREVILLY, by Nadar
A French dandy who thought real dandies were English

OSCAR WILDE
Not all dandies
have been gay

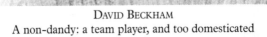

DAVID BECKHAM
A non-dandy: a team player, and too domesticated

JARVIS COCKER
Cool and clever
© All Action

POP DANDIES

LIAM GALLAGHER
Not always
aiming to please
© Brian Rasic/Rex
Features

TRACEY EMIN
The art-dandy
© Harry Borden/Catz Pictures

JOHN MALKOVICH
A film-star dandy

that one of the future Dandy's earliest memories was of the breath of these gifted and charming men on his head.

They were like fairy gifts, but they endowed him with only half their powers, the most ephemeral of their faculties. No doubt it was through hearing and seeing their minds at work, these glories of the human intellect who conducted the most casual conversation as if it were political discourse, and whose humour was the equal of their eloquence, that the young Brummell developed the faculties that were already within him and were to make him (to use the English term) one of the leading conversationalists of his country.

He was sixteen when his father died in 1794. In 1790 he had been sent to Eton, and had already distinguished himself by what was to characterise him so eminently later, and went beyond the sphere of his studies. The care he devoted to his appearance, and his cool, languid manner earned him a name amongst the other pupils that was in vogue at the time. The term Dandy being not yet fashionable, the despots of style were called *Bucks** or *Macaronies*, and he was known as *Buck Brummell*. To judge by the testimony of his contemporaries no one exerted a greater influence on his companions at Eton, with the possible exception of George Canning — though Canning's influence was due to his intelligence and his passion, whereas Brummell's stemmed from less intoxicating faculties. He was proof of Machiavelli's dictum that "The world belongs to cool heads." From Eton he went on to

* *Buck means male in English. It is not the word that matters, since it does not translate, but the sense.*

Oxford where he enjoyed the kind of success for which he was destined. The delight he gave people was not intellectual, and his brand of superiority lay less in laborious mental deliberations than in human relations. On leaving Oxford three months after his father's death, he enlisted as cornet in the 10th Hussars, under the command of the Prince of Wales.

People have gone to great lengths to explain the lively interest Brummell at once inspired in the Prince, and anecdotes have been told that are not worth repeating. Why bother with such gossip? There is a better explanation. Given that Brummell was who he was, how could he fail to attract the attention and affections of the man who was said to take greater pride and satisfaction in the distinction of his manners than in the eminence of his rank? His youthful bloom is as well known as the lengths he went to in order to preserve it. The Prince was thirty-two at the time. His were the heavyset good looks of the house of Hanover, which he sought to lighten through his finery, to quicken them in the fiery light of diamonds. Scrofulous as he was in soul as in body he had nevertheless lost none of his graciousness, that last virtue of courtiers. The future George IV recognised in Brummell something of himself, the part that had remained healthy and radiant, and that was the secret of the favour he showed him.

It was as simple as the conquest of a woman. For are there not friendships that originate in physical things, in external grace, just as there is love that springs from the secret, intangible charms of the soul? Such was the friendship of the Prince of Wales for the young cornet in the Hussars. It was a feeling that arose from the senses, perhaps the only kind that could take root in the depths of that corpulent soul whose body threatened to swallow it up.

His inconstant favour settled on Brummell's head with the unpredictability of caprice and the frenzy of infatuation, just as it was to settle on Lord Barrymore, G. Hanger and so many others. His presentation took place on the famous terrace at Windsor, in the presence of the most exacting people of fashion, and he displayed all the qualities the Prince of Wales must have prized most: extreme youth enhanced by the self-possession of a man who knew how the world worked and who intended to master it, a bold yet infinitely subtle combination of irreverence and respect, and finally an inspired dress sense, all of them supplemented by an unfailing wit. A success of this kind involved something more than sheer extravagance on both sides. The word *extravagance* is used by baffled moralists in the way *nerves* is used by doctors. From this moment on, Brummell found that he ranked high in society's opinion. The son of a humble esquire, a private secretary whose grandfather had been a merchant, was given preference over the noblest names in all England to fill the role of best man to the heir presumptive on the occasion of his wedding to Caroline of Brunswick. Such extreme distinction ensured that he was at once on the most familiar footing with the aristocracy of the salons: Lord R.E. Somerset, Lord Petersham,* Charles Ker, Charles and Robert Manners.

---

* *To those who suffer from myopia, a model of Dandyism, but to those who are not taken in by appearances, no more of a Dandy than a very well-dressed woman is an elegant one.*

Nothing surprising in that, and Brummell was happy. He was born, as the English put it, with a silver spoon in his mouth. He had in his favour that mysterious thing we call a *guiding star*, which regulates lives without reason or justice, but what is more surprising, and what justifies his happiness, is that he fixed the star in its course. The child spoiled by fortune was to be spoiled by society. Byron mentions somewhere a portrait of Napoleon in his imperial coat, and adds, "he seemed to have been born in it." One could say the same of Brummell and of the famous dress coat he invented. His reign began without difficulty, without hesitation, and with a confidence that does the work of a conscience. Everything conspired to strengthen his strange power, and no one opposed it. In a world where personal relations matter more than merit, and where individuals, in order simply to exist, find themselves behaving more like shells than men, Brummell had in his train, as admirers rather than rivals, the most distinguished people in politics and society: the Dukes of York and Cambridge, the Counts of Westmorland and Chatham (William Pitt's brother), the Duke of Rutland, Lord Delamere.

Women, who like priests always range themselves on the side of the strongest, sounded fanfares of admiration from their vermilion lips. They were the trumpets of his glory, but trumpets they remained. Herein lay Brummell's originality, and this is where he differed fundamentally from Richelieu and from almost all men whose behaviour is fundamentally geared to seduction. He was not what is known as a libertine. Richelieu, for his part, was a little too much like the Tartar conquerors who made their beds from the intertwined bodies of women. Brummell collected none of these spoils of war and victory trophies, and his vanity did not immerse itself in the hot blood of passion. The Sirens, daughters of the sea with irresistible voices, were dangerously alluring, but their waists were covered in impenetrable scales.

His vanity did not suffer from this in any way, rather the opposite, since it never found itself in collision with a passion that opposed it, counterbalanced it. It ruled alone, and was the stronger for it.* To love, even in its least elevated sense, means to desire, which means being dependent, a slave to one's desire. However tenderly the arms may be folded about you they nevertheless form a chain, and if you are Richelieu, or for that matter Don Juan himself, when you escape those tender arms you are never breaking more than a single link in the chain you wear. This was the slavery from which Brummell was free. His triumphs were insolent because they were disinterested, and he never became giddy from the heads he turned. In a country like England, where pride and cowardice combine to turn modesty into prudery, there was a certain piquancy in seeing a man, a young man moreover who brought together in his person the charms of society as well as those of nature, stop at the frontier of flirtation, a boundary

---

*   *Affectation can lead to dryness. A Dandy's manners are too good not to be simple, yet he will always be a little affected. His affectation however is extremely refined, reminiscent of the distinctly artificial talent possessed by Mlle Mars. If one were truly passionate one would be too real to be a Dandy. Alfieri could never have been one, and Byron was a Dandy only on certain days.*

women had not set up to be respected, and punish them for their false pretensions. And yet this was how Brummell behaved, not in a calculated way, and without the smallest effort. As anyone who knows anything about women will understand, all this merely redoubled his attraction. He wounded the romantic pride of many a high falutin' lady, while corrupting it with impossible dreams.

So it was that the king of fashion had no official mistress. A more accomplished Dandy than the Prince of Wales, he needed no Mrs Fitzherbert. He was a sultan with no handkerchief. No illusions of the heart or upheavals of the senses coloured his judgements, making them unpredictable or excitable. So his judgement remained sovereign. At the time a word from George Bryan Brummell was decisive, be it praise or blame, and he was the autocrat of opinion. Imagine for the sake of argument that such a man, such power, had been possible in Italy! No woman who was truly in love would have spared him a thought, yet in England the minds of the most besotted, even as they positioned a flower in their hair or tried on an ornament, were far more concerned with Brummell's judgement than with their lover's pleasure.

A duchess (and we all know what kind of airs and graces a title allows you in London salons) would tell her daughters in the thick of a ball, at the risk of being overheard, to be sure to take the utmost care over their posture, their movements and responses should Mr Brummell by any chance be kind enough to address them. For in this first phase of his life he would still mingle with the crowds of dancers at these balls, where the most delectable hands remained idle as they awaited his. Intoxicated with the exceptional position in society he had created himself, later on he renounced this dancer's role as too vulgar for him. Instead he would stand for just a few minutes at the entrance to a ball, then, casting an eye over it, give his verdict in a single word and disappear, thus applying Dandyism's famous principle: "In society, stay as long as you need to make an impression; and as soon as you have made it, move on." He was well aware of his dazzling prestige, and in his case the impression took no time to make.

With such success, such command over society's opinion, such extreme youth to enhance his fame, and his air of charm and cruelty that women both revile and adore, there is no doubt that he inspired many conflicting passions — heartfelt loves as well as implacable hatreds. Yet no trace of them has survived.*

English cant repressed any cries from the soul, assuming anyone would have dared to utter them. In England, propriety renders the heart impotent, which makes it rather difficult for any Mme. de Lespinasse to see the light of day. As for a Caroline Lamb, Brummell never possessed one, for the

---

* *There was talk of Lady J...y, whom he is alleged to have spirited away from the Regent, as the suitably light-hearted saying goes. But Lady J...y remained his friend, and love that ends in friendship is a thing more wondrous than beautiful women who end in the tail of a fish. A poet has cleft through the illusions of the well-meaning hearts of men with a deft stroke of his hatchet: "As long as two people are lovers, they are not friends; when they are no longer lovers, the last thing they will be is friends."*

simple reason that women are more susceptible to betrayal than to indifference.

To our knowledge only one woman has left any of those words about Brummell that both conceal passion and reveal it, and that is the courtesan Harriette Wilson; which is perfectly natural, since she was more jealous of his reputation than of his heart. The qualities that went to make the power of Brummell would have made a courtesan's fortune. Moreover, without being Henriette Wilsons, women are well skilled in making exceptions in favour of their sex! They are endowed with as much mathematical and other forms of genius as men, and they cannot forgive Sheridan the impertinence of having had his hands sculpted as the most beautiful in the whole of England.

X

Alcibiades may have been the most handsome of brilliant generals, but George Bryan Brummell did not possess the military spirit, and did not spend long in the 10th Hussars. His purpose in enlisting may have been more serious than was thought — namely to gain proximity to the Prince of Wales and to establish the personal relationship that quickly brought him to prominence. It has been said, somewhat scornfully, that military uniforms must have carried an irresistible fascination for Brummell, but that is to explain a Dandy in terms of the instincts of a second lieutenant. A Dandy, who places his personal stamp on everything and who cannot exist without a "certain exquisite originality"* (Lord Byron), must necessarily despise uniforms.

* *This word can only be used by an Englishman. Originality*

Moving to more serious matters than this question of uniforms, it was fundamental to Brummell's nature that he should be misjudged once his influence had passed. During his lifetime even those who resisted it were subject to it, and given contemporary prejudice the analysis of such a person today is a difficult piece of psychology. Women will never forgive him for having as elegant a manner as themselves, men for not having it as much as he did. The point has already been made, but we will not tire of repeating it: the thing that really makes a Dandy is independence. Otherwise there would be a set of rules on how to be a Dandy, and there is no such thing.*

Every Dandy is endowed with audacity, but his boldness is combined with tact, so that he will always exercise restraint

---

* *If there were, one could be a Dandy simply by observing the rules, in which case anyone could be one: all they would need to do would be to follow the prescription. Unfortunately for our young people, it is not quite like that. There are undoubtedly a few general principles and traditions governing Dandyism, but set against the importance of caprice they are nothing, and the exercise of caprice is only permitted to those to whom it is suited, and who sanctify it through use.*

has no home in France, where it is denied warmth and water, and hated because it is seen as an aristocratic prerogative. It incites mediocre people against those who are other than themselves, and who are always ready and willing to gnash their teeth at them impotently, and to froth at the mouth. Be like everyone else is the equivalent maxim for men to the one crammed into young girls' heads: IT IS ESSENTIAL TO BE WELL THOUGHT OF (from the Marriage of Figaro).

and unerringly home in on the point, famously identified by Pascal, where originality and eccentricity intersect. It is for this reason that Brummell could not adapt to the constraints of military regulations, which are a kind of uniform in themselves. From that point of view, he made an appalling officer. Mr Jesse, an admirable chronicler though one who does not forget enough, has several anecdotes to tell about his hero's lack of discipline. He breaks ranks during manoeuvres and disobeys his colonel's orders, but since the colonel is under his spell, he does not reprimand him. After three years Brummell is made a captain. Then suddenly his regiment is garrisoned in Manchester, and for that reason alone the youngest captain in the army's finest regiment resigns his commission.

He told the Prince of Wales that he was unwilling to be separated from him, which was more tactful than any mention of London, for it was the thought of leaving London that held him back. It was there that his celebrity had been established, a celebrity that was indigenous to its salon life, where wealth, leisure and the finest degree of civilisation produced the charming affectations that had taken the place of nature. For the pearl of Dandyism to be dropped in industrial Manchester would be as monstrous a notion as that of Rivarol living in Hamburg!

He rescued his future reputation by staying in London. He took lodgings in Chesterfield Street, at no. 4, opposite George Selwyn — one of the stars of fashion whose light he had dimmed. His material wealth, considerable though it was, in no way measured up to his position. Others, many others, among these sons of Lords and Nabobs, enjoyed a level of luxury that would have put his own in the shade, if people without a thought in their heads could be said to overshadow a thinking man. The splendour of Brummell was intellectual rather than opulent. He was one more proof of the good sense of the man who is content to leave the colour scarlet to savages, and he was later to come up with this great axiom of dress: "To be well-dressed you must not be noticed." Bryan Brummell had fine horses, an excellent cook and kept house like a woman with poetic aspirations, where he gave delicious dinners at which the guests were as choice as the wines.* Like all his countrymen, particularly then, he tended to drink to the point of intoxication.

At once apathetic and highly strung, surrounded by the tedium and indolence of English existence from which Dandyism only partially escapes, he sought the emotions of that other life where the pulse beats faster and the colours dazzle — a life that is found in the bottom of a glass. But even as he descended into the swirling depths of drunkenness he remained master of his wit and his elegance, as did Sheridan, to whom we keep reverting because he was the font of every form of superiority.

And it was here that the source of his dominance lay. Methodist preachers (and they are not confined to England)

---

* *Everyone drank, from the busiest to the most leisured, from the salon lazzaroni (the Dandies) to government ministers. To drink like Pitt and Dundas is still a proverb. When Pitt drank his great soul filled with love of England, though not to repletion, and what he really thirsted for was variety. Strong men often try to escape from themselves. Sadly, nature does not always allow them.*

and similar purblind folk who have had their say on Brummell have depicted him as a kind of dummy with no brain or guts. Nothing could be wider of the mark. To belittle the man still more they have attempted to belittle the age in which he lived, claiming that it shared his follies. They are wasting their time and effort! They can hammer away all they like at an era that was glorious for Great Britain, just as in Florence they hammered away at the gold sphere that held the water they were attempting to compress. But the rebel element burst through its confines rather than submit, and they will not succeed in reducing English society from 1794 to 1816 to nothing more than an age of decadence.

There are some eras that refuse to be compressed and resist whatever people say of them. Are we to believe that the great era of Pitt, Fox, Wyndham, Byron, and Walter Scott, suddenly contracts because it included the name Brummell! The reason such a claim is so absurd is precisely because Brummell had something about him that was capable of attracting and fixing the gaze on a magnificent epoch — the kind of gaze that does not allow itself to be fooled, like birds before a mirror, simply by the lure of elegant or ostentatious clothes.

As it happens Brummell, the object of this fascinated gaze, attached far less importance to the art of personal appearance, as practised by the great Chatham, than has been thought.* His tailors Davidson and Meyer have been credited, stupidly and insolently, with being the fathers of his glory, yet they

---

*   *The only historical figure to have been great without being simple.*

were far from holding the place in his life they have been allotted. We would do better to heed Lister, whose portrait is a faithful one: "He scorned to share his fame with his tailor, finding it much better to trust alone to the nameless grace of polished ease."

It is true that his career began at a time when the democratic Charles Fox was introducing red heels on to English carpets, apparently as a fashion item, and given his interest in external effects Brummell must have concerned himself with fashion in all its aspects. He was not unaware that dress exerts a latent though positive influence on those who are the first to disdain it from the majestic height of their immortal wit. Later however, as Lister tells us, he shed this youthful preoccupation, though without dispensing with what he had learned from experience and observation. He remained impeccably groomed, but he subdued the colours of his clothes, simplified their cut, and wore them without thinking about it.*

In so doing he reached the summit of an art that works hand in hand with nature. The means he used to create an impression were of the highest breeding, a point all too often forgotten. He has been thought of as a purely physical being, when in fact even the kind of beauty he possessed was intellectual, and his attraction lay not so much in the

---

* *As though they were accidental! A Dandy can spend ten hours dressing, but once it is done, he will put it out of his mind. It is for others to notice how well-dressed he is.*

regularity of his features as in his physiognomy as a whole. His hair was almost reddish, like Alfieri's, and a riding accident during a charge had marred the Grecian line of his profile. The way he held his head was more handsome than his face, and his bearing — the physiognomy of the body — was even more impressive than its physical perfection. As Lister writes, "He was neither handsome nor ugly, but there was in his whole person an expression of finesse and concentrated irony, and his eyes were extraordinarily penetrating."

Sometimes there came into those clever eyes a look of glacial indifference without contempt, as becomes a consummate Dandy, a man who bears within him something superior to the visible world. His splendid voice made the English language as beautiful to hear as to read or ponder. "He did not pretend to be short-sighted," says Lister again, "but when those present were not of sufficient importance to suit his vanity, he would assume that calm and wandering gaze which examines without recognition, neither fixes itself nor will be fixed, is not interested or diverted by anything." Such a man was George Bryan Brummell, the *Beau.* The present writer, who devotes these pages to him, saw him in his old age, and it was clear what he had been in his most dazzling years. For a man's facial expression lies beyond wrinkles' reach, and a man whose main distinction lies in his physiognomy is a good deal less mortal than others.

Moreover what his physiognomy promised his intellect more than delivered. It was not for nothing that a heavenly light seemed to play about his frame. Yet it would be unfair to deny his intelligence simply because, being of an infinitely rare kind, it refused to devote itself to the things that dominate that of other men. He was a great artist in his way, only his art was not particularised, not executed at any given time. His art was his life itself, the ceaseless sparkling of faculties not given to men who are born to live with people like themselves. Where others gave pleasure with their works, he did so with his person. His value lay in his presence. He drew from its torpor a society that was horribly sated and wordly-wise, and a prey to all the emotional fatigue of ancient civilisations — a difficult task if ever there was one, and he did so without sacrificing an ounce of his own dignity.*

His every whim was respected. Not Etherege, nor Cibber, nor Congreve, nor Vanbrugh could insert a character like him into their plays, since he was beyond the reach of ridicule. He did not avoid it by tactfulness, or defy it by his coolness. His guarantee against it was sheer wit — a shield with a spike in its centre, capable of turning defence into aggression.

Here perhaps he will be easier to understand. People who are least sensitive to insinuating elegance can feel the sustained force of power, and Brummell's hold over his era becomes less mysterious, less inexplicable, when one realises

---

* *Without shedding his own. Amiability involves too much activity and too much directness for a Dandy ever to be amiable exactly. A Dandy never has a need or a care for anything. If some have gone so far as to say that Brummell was amiable on certain evenings, it is just that the coquetry of powerful men, even when it is mediocre, is irresistible. They are like beautiful women to whom one feels grateful for anything (at least when one is a man).*

the power of his mockery, something which has been insufficiently realised till now. Irony is a gift that dispenses with all others. It confers on a man a sphinx-like air, as absorbing as mystery, as troubling as danger.* Now Brummell had this gift and deployed it in a way that could pierce a man's self-esteem, even whilst he appeared to massage it. It was a gift that redoubled the myriad interests of a superior conversation by making the vanities of those involved feel insecure — a condition that does not of itself inspire wit, but stimulates it in those who possess it and quickens the pulse of those who do not.

It was the gift of irony that made him the greatest hoaxer England has ever had. "No keeper of a menagerie", says the author of *Granby,* "could better show off a monkey than he could an original. He could ingeniously cause the unconscious subject to place his own absurdites in the best point of view." A somewhat cruel sort of amusement, it might be thought, but Dandyism is the product of a bored society, and boredom makes you bad.

In judging Brummell it is important never to lose sight of this. He was first and foremost a Dandy, our theme is confined to the power he wielded, and it is a strange tyranny that never induced revolt! Like all Dandies, he preferred to

* *"You are a palace within a labyrinth",* wrote a woman who wanted to look without seeing, and seek without finding, unaware that she was expressing a principle of Dandyism. The truth is, not just anyone can be a palace, whereas one can always be a labyrinth.

shock rather than to be liked — a very human preference, but one that can easily lead men astray, for the most exquisite shock of all is horror. Once on that slope, where do you stop? Only Brummell knew the answer. He dispensed terror and warmth in precisely equal doses, and with them he brewed the magic potion of his influence. His indolence would not permit him to display verve, because to possess verve is to show enthusiasm, to show enthusiasm is to care about something, and to care about something is to admit inferiority. He possessed an abundance of self-control and kept a close watch on himself. He was as trenchant in conversation as Hazlitt was in his writings. His witticisms crucified,* and yet his impertinence was too thorough-going to be condensed and contained in epigrams alone.

---

* *He did not throw out witticisms, he let them drop. A Dandy's wit never flickers or scintillates. It does not move like quicksilver or darting flame like that of a Casanova, for example, or a Beaumarchais. He may come up with the same lines on different occasions, but he will deliver them differently.*

Dandies represent the unpredictable in a highly stratified and structured society, and yet they are obliged, however well protected they are against it, to inhale the ghastly germs of Puritanism. They inhabit the tower of the Plague, and such a dwelling place is bound to be insalubrious. That is why they speak so much of dignity, and perhaps they think it undignified to indulge in furious bursts of repartee. They live on the idea of dignity as if impaled on it — a posture that impinges a little on one's freedom of movement, and obliges one, however supple one is, to hold oneself a little too rigidly.

It was reflected in his words, his acts, his attitude, his gestures and in the very sound of his voice. In a word, he used it with the unquestionable superiority it requires if it is to be accepted among people of breeding. For impertinence borders on rudeness the way the sublime borders on the ridiculous, and should it stray beyond nuance, all is lost. The spirit of Impertinence goes about semi-veiled, and does not rely on words to display itself. Its power is penetrating, without being heavy-handed, in a manner quite different from the most brilliantly framed epigram.

When you have it, it is the best guarantee of respect against the vanity of others, so often hostile to your own; it is equally the most elegant cloak beneath which to hide the failings one senses in oneself. Those who possess it have little need for anything else. Did not impertinence do more for the reputation of Prince Talleyrand as a wit than his wit itself? A child of Self-confidence and Levity — qualities that may appear mutually exclusive — it is also a sister to Grace, to whom she must remain forever bound. The beauty of both is enhanced by the contrast between them. Indeed, without Impertinence, would Grace not be too much of a vapid blonde, and without Grace, would not Impertinence be an excessively pert brunette? To be truly themselves the two must be intermingled.

And this is what George Bryan Brummell did better than anyone. This man, who has been too superficially judged, was so intellectual a force that he ruled more by his aura than by his words. His effect on people was more immediate than any produced by language alone. He produced it by an intonation, a look, a gesture, by deliberate intention, even by silence,* and this could explain why he left so few witticisms behind. Moreover to judge by the examples the memoirists of the time have left us, to us they seem either lacking in savour, or have too much, which is another way of having too little. In them one senses the tart, salty genius of a people who go in for boxing and drinking, yet somehow avoid vulgarity, even where we Frenchmen would cease to be delicate. When you think of it, what is invariably called *wit* is the product of the mind, and has to do essentially with language, with customs and social life, things that vary most from one people to another, and are doomed to wither on foreign soil, in the exile of translation. Even the words that characterise it for each nation cannot be translated in their full sense.

Try finding for example the equivalent of wit, humour, or

---

* *He enjoyed conversation too much not to remain silent often, but his silence did not have the depth of the following writer: "They watched me to see whether I understood their ideas on this and that, or their views on whomsoever. But they probably took me for some salon mediocrity, and for my part I revelled in the opinion I imagined they had of my person. It made me think of kings who like to stay incognito." This kind of proud, solitary self-consciousness must be unknown to Dandies, and Brummell's silence was yet another way of creating an impression. It was the teasing coquetry of people who are certain of their charm, and who know how to go about kindling desire.*

fun, the three elements that go to make up the originality of the English mind. Everything that is individual is volatile, and wit does not carry across from one language to another, any more than poetry, which at least is inspired by universal sentiments. As with certain wines which do not travel well, it is best drunk on its own territory. Nor does it age well; like the most beautiful roses it is soon past, which is perhaps the secret of the pleasure it gives. Another case where God has compensated for the brevity of life by its intensity, in order that the love of perishable things should not be lost to our hearts.

So Brummell's witticisms will not be quoted. They would not live up to his reputation, even though they deserve to do so. The circumstances in which they shot forth, which gave them their electric charge so to speak, no longer exist. Let us not disturb these grains of sand which once flew like sparks, and which time has dispersed after extinguishing them, by seeking to count them up. Thanks to the diversity of our vocations, there are some moments of glory that are now no more than sounds in silence, which make us despair of thought and forever nourish our reveries.

Yet how can we fail to marvel at this wave of glory descending on a man as practically-minded as Brummell — practical in three senses since he was vain, English and a Dandy! Like all practical people who live close to themselves and whose faith and will are devoted to instant pleasures, Brummell had no thought for anything but them, and enjoyed them in profusion. Fate rewarded him in the currency he valued most. Society gave him all the good fortune it can offer, and for him no happiness could be greater.* For unlike Byron — who was a renegade of Dandyism at one moment, and a recidivist the next — he did not believe that the world is not worth a single one of the joys it takes away.

From his permanently intoxicated vanity the world took nothing. From 1799 almost until 1814, there was no party in London, no festivity where the presence of the great Dandy was not regarded as a triumph or his absence a catastrophe. The newspapers printed his name in advance at the head of the most illustrious guests. At balls thrown by Almack, at Ascott meetings, everyone bowed to his dictatorship. He was the leading light of the Watier club, of which Byron was a member, along with Lords Alvanley, Mildmay and Pierrepoint, and the soul (if soul is the word) of the famous Brighton Pavilion, of Carlton House, of Belvoir.

He was especially close to Sheridan, the Duchess of York, Erskine, Lord Townshend and the passionate and singular Duchess of Devonshire, a poetess in three languages whose patrician lips embraced the London butchers to steal votes from Fox, which meant that he was able to impose himself at

---

* *Was he satisfied with the only form of happiness that is pitiable? moralists will ask insultingly. And why shouldn't he be? Satisfied vanity can fill a man's life as much as satisfied love. Whereas boredom, God help us, boredom is the straw which can break the best-tempered steel of happiness. It is at the basis of everything, for everyone, and even more so for the Dandy, the kind of man of whom it has been said, ingeniously but depressingly: "They surrounded themselves with life's every pleasure, but in the way that a stone accumulates moss and so ceases to be penetrated by the freshness of its surface."*

the level of those who were in a position to judge him. Had he really been no more than the royal favourite of the moment they would soon have discovered the emptiness under the exalted profile. It is said that Mme de Staël was almost desolate not to have pleased him. The all-powerful coquetry of her wit was endlessly held at bay by the endless humour and frigid soul of the Dandy, this capricious, unmelting man who had his own good reasons for making fun of excessive enthusiasm in any form.

Corinne came to grief with Brummell as she had with Bonaparte: a parallel which reminds us of Lord Byron's remark mentioned above. He had an even more original conquest: that of Lady Stanhope, the amazonian Arab who galloped off from European civilisation and English routine — that battered old roundabout — to revive her sensations in the dangers and independence of the desert. And of all the civilised folk she had left behind the only one she could remember after many years' absence was perhaps the most civilised of all — the Dandy, George Brummell.

When one makes a tally of the keen and lasting impressions he left on the most prominent personages of the era one is bound to treat the man who produced them, whether we think him a fop or not, with the seriousness we owe to everything that conquers man's imagination. Poets, if only because they reflect their times, were saturated with Brummell. Moore sang his praises — though what is Moore?*

---

* *Irish sentimentality apart, the poet of pink paper mâché.*

Unbeknown to its author, Brummell may have been one of the Muses who inspired *Don Juan*. In any event this strange poem has an essentially Dandyish tone from one end to the other, and powerfully illuminates the cast and quality of Brummell's mind. It was his most evanescent aspects that raised him high on the horizon and kept him there. He was never to descend from it, though he did fall, bringing down with him something that, in its perfection, has never reappeared since his time, except in debased form. The stupefying life of the Turf has replaced Dandyism, and nothing is left of High Life except jockeys and whippers of dogs.*

* *There was d'Orsay, but d'Orsay, this lion amongst men of fashion, as beautiful as those who roam the Atlas mountains, was not a Dandy. People got him wrong. His was an infinitely more complex nature, larger and more human than this very English thing. It has been said many times but we must keep coming back to it: a lymphatic disposition, a kind of stagnant water that only froths when it is whipped up by Vanity, is the physiological base of the Dandy, and d'Orsay had the red corpuscles of France. He was a sinewy, full-blooded fellow with broad shoulders, a François I chest and an appealing beauty. His handshake was superb without being arrogant, and he had a way of tending it that that stole people's hearts away! So unlike the haughty handshake of the Dandy. D'Orsay was so naturally and passionately pleasing to everyone that even men went about wearing his locket, while Dandies only made men wear you know what, and made women like them by displeasing them. (Never forget this nuance when it comes to judging them.)*

Finally, d'Orsay was a master of amiable benevolence, and benevolence is a feeling completely unknown to Dandies. True, he practised the art of the toilette as much as them, in which he was profound rather than ostentatious, and this is no doubt the reason that superficial people saw him as the successor to Brummell. But Dandyism is not simply the art of knowing how to tie a cravat, indeed some Dandies have never even worn them, and Byron, with his wondrous neck, was an example! On the other hand d'Orsay was a genuine artist. The hand that he was in the habit of offering too much — since coquetry works more by what it refuses than what it accords — also sculpted, while Brummell merely painted his fans for insincere faces and empty heads. The marbles d'Orsay left have a thoughtful quality, and to his talent for sculpture we must add the fact that he almost became a writer. At twenty-three years old he was thought worthy of that letter of Byron to Alfred D... that is to be found in the famous memoirs where Moore was cowardly enough to replace names by asterisks and juicy anecdotes by dots... (An amiable fellow, this Moore!) Conceited he may have been, but d'Orsay was loved by the most conceited women of his time. This leaves aside the unaffected ones, of whom there are only two or three every century; so why speak of them? He even inspired a lasting passion that will remain historic. Dandies, for their part, are only loved in fits and starts. Women hate them but give themselves to them happily enough, so that Dandies can enjoy a sensation worth any amount of pounds sterling: that of pressing hatreds in their arms. As regards that charming duel of d'Orsay's, where he threw his plate at the head of an officer who had spoken badly of the Virgin Mary, and fought for her because she was a woman and he could not tolerate lack of respect for a woman in his presence, what could be less Dandy and more French?

XI

In a story that is made up of impressions rather than facts we shall pass swiftly over the disappearance of the meteor at the end of this incredible novel (it is far more than a tale), in which London society was the heroine and Brummell the hero. In truth the end was a long time coming. Lacking facts — the historical measure of time — let us use dates, and judge the profundity of his influence by its duration. From 1793 to 1816 is twenty-two years. In the moral as in the physical world, what is airy and light is easily displaced. A success that continued over so many years shows that Brummell's existence answered a human need in the social circumstances of the time. Even when he was later obliged to leave England, the interest that centred on his person was not exhausted.

The enthusiasm he inspired did not desert him. In 1812 and 1813 he was more powerful than ever, despite the damage gambling had wreaked on the material fortune that underpinned his life of elegance. He was in truth a great gambler. There is no need to examine whether this boldness before the unknown, this thirst for adventure that makes gamblers and pirates, was to be found in his own temperament or in the tendencies of the people he associated with. What is certain is that English society is more greedy for emotions than for guineas, and that the only way to dominate a society is to espouse its passions.

If there was another reason besides his gambling losses for his fall into decline, it appears to have been his quarrel with the Prince who had loved him and had been, in a manner of speaking, his courtier. The Regent was getting old. He had grown an embonpoint, that polyp which kills beauty gradually, by soft embraces. With his implacable sense of humour and the tiger's pride that success implants in men's hearts, Brummell had once or twice mocked the Prince's efforts to repair the damage of time, in the way a coquette seeks to preserve her failing powers, and which made him look ridiculous.

At Carlton House there was a concierge of monstrous corpulence whose nickname was Big Ben, and Brummell transferred the sobriquet from valet to master. Mrs Fitzherbert he called Benina. Such bold and derisory talk could not but cut these proud souls to the quick, and Mrs Fitzherbert was not alone amongst the women who surrounded the Prince of Wales in finding Brummell's ironic familiarity offensive. Such was the real cause of the disgrace into which the great Dandy suddenly fell.

The first explanation — the story of the bell — appears to

be apocryphal.* In doing his best to refute it, Mr Jesse does not rely solely on Brummell's denial, but rightly points to the "vulgar impudence" the story reveals; impudence was often present in the Dandy, but vulgarity never. In any event a single isolated fact, however revealing, is not as serious, in terms of a motive for disgrace, as the thousands of sharp-tongued slings and sallies thrown off by Brummell in his most frivolous manner, and aimed at the Regent's liaisons. What the husband of Caroline of Brunswick had tolerated was not to be borne by the lover of Mrs Fitzherbert and Lady Connyngham.†

And even if he had borne it, and the male favourite had got away with wounding the females, the Prince would never have suffered attacks on his physical self, his own ego, without resentment. Brummell's famous "Who's your fat

---

* *Here it is. In order to win a highly disrespectful bet, at dinner one evening Brummell indicated the bell and gave the Prince of Wales the order: "Ring, George!" The Prince is said to have obeyed, and to have told the servant who entered, pointing to Brummell: "Take this drunkard to his bed."*

† *Brummell's influence, even his jokes, had a lot to do with the alienation of Caroline of Brunswick from the Prince of Wales. We know that the famous wedding night, which the Prince spent on a carpet next to the fire while his young wife waited for him under the ostrich feathers of the nuptial bed, had been preceded by a dinner with the Dandies. These practical men disliked the vaporous sentimentalism which Caroline had brought in her German woman's baggage, and which manifested itself a little later. Moreover she was the Prince's legitimate wife, in a country of official conjugal*

friend?", uttered publicly in Hyde Park while indicating His Royal Highness, and a host of similar quips, explain things far better than this absence of decorum, justified, moreover, by a bet.

Yet at this stage (1813) neither the resentful estrangement of the Prince nor his gambling losses had shaken Brummell's position. The hand that had raised him up precipitated his fall by withdrawing its support. The salons remained faithful, but it was not enough. It was a bitter thing for the Regent to see a half-ruined Dandy engaged in a struggle for influence with himself, the most elevated personage in Great Britain. Anacreon-Archiloque Moore, who did not always write on powder-blue paper, and whose Irish hatreds sometimes helped him hit on the phrase that skewers the most effectively, put the following verses in the mouth of the Prince of Wales. They

happiness where the women poured the tea! With its love of the unpredictable and hatred of the small-minded pedantries of domestic servants, Dandyism prefers all the problems of mistresses to the imperturbable public happiness of Lord and Lady Grey, for example, so lauded by Mme de Staël. English Dandies, obliged to live cheek by jowl with these legal felicities, did not and could not share the opinion of Mme de Staël, who incidentally could have encountered few examples of such felicities in the salons of Paris. Distance makes poetic, and the imagination is in constant need of dreams to caress. But when the woman who depicted herself in Corinne as being in love with D, who was in love with C, who loved T, pours caresses on this one, she is less truthful to the heart and to the imagination than the Dandies, and reduces herself to the point of being nothing more than the daughter of Mme Necker.

were addressed to the Duke of York, but were widely quoted:

> Neither feel I resentments, nor wish there should come ill
> To mortal — except (now I think on't) Beau Brummell,
> Who threatened last year, in a superfine passion,
> To cut *me* and bring the old King into fashion.

These insulting verses surely justify the words used by the king of Dandies about the Royal Dandy in conversation with Colonel MacMahon: "I have made him what he is, and I can easily unmake him." Are they not also conclusive proof of how much the power over opinion exercised by this Warwick of elegance belonged to him in his own right, and of how independent and sovereign he was?

Even more striking proof of this power came in this same year, 1813. The Watier club was preparing a great party, and seriously debated whether or not to invite the Prince of Wales, simply because he had quarrelled with Brummell. Brummell, who knew how to give his most generous gestures a tinge of impertinence, had to insist firmly that the Prince be invited. No doubt he was more than happy to see *chez lui* (he was a member of the club) the host he no longer saw at Carlton House, and to arrange for this face to face to take place in the presence of the entire gilded youth of England.

But the Prince, not at his best on the occasion, forgot his claims to be an accomplished gentleman, while also failing to remember the duties that hospitality imposes on those who receive it. Brummell, who was ready to meet Dandyism with Dandyism, responded to his sulky air with that elegant coolness that he wore like armour and which rendered him invincible.* Of all the clubs of England it was precisely this Watier club where gambling mania was at its most intense. There were appalling scandals. Drunk on port and ginger, these world-weary creatures, devoured by spleen, came there every night to rid themselves of the mortal ennui of their lives and to stir their Normans' blood — a blood that only boils when they are engaged in pillage — by risking the most magnificent fortunes on a throw of the dice.

Brummell, as noted, was the star of this celebrated club, which he would not have been had he not plunged into the thick of the gambling and the bets. The truth is that he was neither more nor less a gambler than those who sought excitement in this charming pandemonium, where vast sums of money were lost with total indifference, which for the Dandies was the equivalent of the grace shown by gladiators who fell in the arena. Many enjoyed long runs of luck, just as he did; but just as many found themselves up against it even longer. Habit and sangfroid had made him a clever player, but he could do nothing against fate, which was to curtail the happiness of his life by the poverty of his last days.

---

*   It might be better perhaps to say that it made him believe himself invulnerable. But Cleopatra's wonderful sigh of lassitude in Shakespeare: "'Tis sweating labour / To bear such idleness so near the heart/ As Cleopatra this." is smothered in the Dandy's breast. These stoics of the boudoir drink their own blood as it flows beneath their mask, and stay masked. For Dandies as for women, to appear is to be.

The arrival in London in 1814 of the Russian and Prussian officers of the armies of Alexander and Blücher stoked up the conflagration of gambling amongst the English. For Brummell, it was the moment of disaster. In his celebrity and social status there was an element of chance which was to sink them both. Like all gamblers he struggled desperately against fate and was overcome. He fell back on usury and was engulfed in debt. It has even been suggested that his dignity went too, but nothing conclusive has been said on the matter. What might have given rise to certain rumours was his dangerous gift of adopting poses which could smack of low behaviour, and sometimes he abused his gift.*

For example when he was in a tight corner he is known to have accepted a quite considerable sum from someone who was anxious to figure amongst the Dandies, by claiming acquaintance with the man they saw as their master. When he asked for the money to be returned, in the middle of a large group of people, Brummell told the

---

* *These qualities have always led astray those who possess them. For example Henri IV, the Duc d'Orléans (the Regent), Mirabeau etc. etc. True, Henri IV had them in small quantity, but the Regent had them copiously and Mirabeau enormously. Mirabeau shook off the mud with as much pride as the Duc d'Orléans met these affronts to his honour with grace and gaiety. Have we not seen him make a joke of kicks in the backside?, and from the goat's foot of Dubois at that. These people, who profaned lovable traits, were more guilty than Brummell, for they were not faced as he was with a Puritan society, which explains every excess and justifies many injuries.*

importunate creditor that he had already paid him. "Paid? When?" the lender asked in astonishment, and Brummell responded in his ineffable manner: "When I said to you 'Jimmy, how are you?' as you passed the window of White's." Such a reply took elegance to the point of cynicism. It does not take many remarks like this to make those who hear them reluctant to go out of their way to be fair to him.

Moreover the moment when the entire world ceases to be fair, the moment of misfortune, was about to strike for Brummell. His ruin was final, and he knew it. With the impassiveness of the Dandy he had calculated, watch in hand, the precise time it was wise to remain on the battle scene, the scene of the most admirable successes a man of fashion had ever enjoyed. He had resolved not to make a spectacle of his humiliation, as he had of his glory, and behaved like those proud coquettes who prefer to abandon the man they love rather than be abandoned by those who do not love them. On 16 May 1816, after dining on a capon sent by Watier, he drank a bottle of Bordeaux.* (Byron had drunk two before replying to the article in the *Edinburgh Revue* attacking his satire on English Bards and Scottish critics). Then he wrote, quite without hope and with the

---

* *Such is the English physiological system. Moral courage is determined like physical courage. The English make bad soldiers when they are not well fed. The glory of Wellington is that he was an excellent army contractor.*

nonchalance of a lost man tempting fate, the letter which has been often quoted:

"My dear Scrope, send me two hundred pounds. The banks are shut and all my money is in the three percents. It shall be repaid tomorrow morning.

Yours,

George Brummell."

The note that came back from Scrope Davies at once was Spartan in its friendship and its laconic style:

"My Dear George, 'tis very unfortunate, but all my money is in the three percents.

Yours,

S. Davies."

Brummell was too much of a Dandy to be wounded by such a reply, and as Mr Jesse cleverly notes, he was not a man to moralise about it. The gambler's love of allowing fate to decide had made him throw a leaf on the waters and the waters had carried it off! The reply from Scrope had been curt to the point of cruelty, but it was not vulgar. Between one Dandy and another honour was safe and sound. The same evening Brummell made his toilette stoically and put in an appearance at the opera. He was a phoenix on its pyre, more beautiful in fact, since he sensed that he would not rise from its ashes. To look at him, who would have said he was a lost man?

After the opera the vehicle he took was a post chaise, and by 17 May he was at Dover. By the 18th he had left England. Some days after his departure the elegant furniture of the Dandy ("man of fashion departed for the Continent") was sold at public auction by order of the Sheriff of Middlesex, according to the record of the sales. The buyers included the most fashionable Londoners and distinguished English aristocrats, including the Duke of York, the Lords Yarmouth and Bessborough, Lady Warburton, Sir H. Smyth, Sir H. Peyton, Sir W. Burgoyne, Colonels Sheddon and Cotton, General Phipps, etc etc.

All of them wanted — and like acquisitive Englishmen who want something they were prepared to pay for it — the precious relics of an exhausted luxury, objects consecrated by a man's taste, fragile, fungible things that Brummell had touched and used. This opulent society, for whom even superfluous things had become necessities, paid most of all for objects that had the least value in themselves, knick-knacks that only exist by virtue of the hand that chose them and the caprice which had given them birth. Brummell was said to have one of the biggest collection of snuff boxes in England, and when one of them was opened inside was found the following note, in his hand: "This box was intended for the Prince Regent, had he conducted himself better with me." The simplicity of the phrasing made it even more impertinent, for it is only petty conceit that is lacking in simplicity.

Arriving in Calais — "the asylum for English debtors" — Brummell did his best to keep the truth at bay: that he was an exile. In his flight he had brought with him some debris of his past magnificence, and the debris of an English fortune amounted almost to a fortune in France. He rented an apartment from a bookseller of the town which he furnished with a sumptuous fantasy, in a way to recall his boudoir in Chesterfield Street or his salons in Chapel Street and Park Lane. His friends (if that is not too sincere a word, since a Dandy's friends are always a little like gallants of friendship) supplied him with the daily expenses for a life that continued to have a certain style.

The Duke and Duchess of York, with whom he had enjoyed closer ties after his break with the Prince of Wales, Mr Chamberlayne and many others, then and later very nobly came to the aid of the unfortunate Beau, so displaying more eloquently than ever the deep impression he had made on all those who knew him. In the same way that writers or public orators are sometimes pensioned by parties whose opinions they represent, so he was given a pension by people he had charmed. In England this generosity had no degrading overtones, and was not new. Had not Chatham received a considerable sum from the ageing Duchess of Marlborough for an oppositionary speech? And Burke himself, who lacked Chatham's breadth of vision and was bombastic in his virtue as well as his eloquence, did he not accept from the Marquis of Rockingham, a minister at the time, a property which rendered him eligible for Parliament?

What was novel was the cause of this generosity. People felt as grateful for a feeling of pleasure as for a service rendered, and they were right to do so, for the greatest service that can be rendered to a bored society is surely to afford it a little amusement.

Even more astonishing than this manifestation of gratitude, always a rare commodity, the Dandy's ascendancy did not end with his absence, and survived his departure. The British salons were as much occupied with Brummell in exile as when he had been there, dictating his commands to a world that could be as submissive towards those who love it as it could be crushing towards those who flee it. Public interest pierced the Channel fog, crossed the sea and reached him on the other side, in the foreign town where he had sought refuge. Fashionable people made many a pilgrimage to Calais, amongst them the Dukes of Wellington, Rutland, Richmond, Beaufort, Bedford, and the Lords Sefton, Jersey, Willoughby d'Eresby, Craven, Ward and Stuart de Rothsay. As splendid as in London, Brummell kept up all the appearances in his style of life. One day Lord Westmorland, who was passing through Calais, sent word that he would be happy to offer him dinner and that the dinner would be at three o'clock. The Beau replied that he never ate at this hour, and turned his Lordship down. He lived the monotonous routine of Englishmen idling on the Continent, his solitude interrupted only by the visits of his compatriots. Though he did not affect the arrogance of the aristocrat or of the misanthrope, his courtesy was so elaborate that it did not attract many of those into whose company fate had thrown him.

He remained a stranger on account of the language, but even more so by the habits of his past.* A Dandy is more insular than an Englishman, for London society is like an island within an island, and in any case those in search of distinction cannot be too free and easy in their ways. Yet for all his proud reserve he was somewhat less resistant to social advances when they were made under the guise of a good dinner.† His taste for good food, as delicate as a flavour and as exacting as a passion, had always been one of the most pronounced aspects of his hedonism. This sensuality, common in intelligent men, made his vanity less intractable. Yet it was his incomparable aplomb that capped everything.

---

* *Everyone knows Scrope Davies' joke, which Byron honoured by mentioning it in a poem: "Like Napoleon in Russia, when Brummell was learning French he was conquered by the elements." A little overstated, perhaps, but then it was a joke. It is true that he spoke our tongue incorrectly and in an anglicised way, like all those whose mouths are more accustomed to chewing anglo-saxon pebbles and to talking next to the sea. Yet his manner of speaking was improved by the aristocratic flavour he gave to the words, if not by their exactness, and his irreproachably gentlemanly manners gave whatever he said a strange and extraneous distinction, a kind of grave though piquant originality which did him no harm.*

† *The Dandy never quite overcomes his original Puritanism. However great their elegance it never acquires the informality of Richelieu's, never goes so far as to forget all reserve. "If you are considerate enough in London you can pass for a foreigner," said the Prince de Ligne.*

"Who is that bowing to you, Sefton?" he said to Lord Sefton when they were taking a walk in public. In fact it was the honest provincial at whose house he was due to dine that evening who was greeting Brummell himself.

He lived in Calais for some years. The high gloss of his vanity, always on display, no doubt disguised many sorrows, of which some were intellectual. Conversation had become impossible for someone who was above all a man of conversation.*

It always needed a spark from someone else's mind to ignite his own, and he was without it; a terrible anguish, familiar to Mme de Staël! The thought that he was renowned

---

* *One may speak several languages, but one only converses in one. For Brummell even Paris would have been no substitute for London. Moreover nowadays Paris is no more a centre of conversation than any other town. There is no real talk any more, and today Mme de Staël would have lost her affection for her "bubbling stream" in the Rue du Bac. In Paris people are too preoccupied with the money they do not have, and think themselves too much the equal of everyone else to talk well. Wit no longer cascades from its windows any more than anything else. In London the idea of making a fortune dominates and excites many a mind, but above a certain level one finds a society which can think about something better. Then there is its system of ranking and of class (whether it is a good or bad thing is not the question here) which both concentrates minds and makes them effervesce. In such a society you need a lot of finesse to be impertinent, and a great deal of graciousness if polite behaviour is to give pleasure! And it is difficulty that makes heroes. In Paris salon life is too easy — no more than a matter of entering and*

as far away as London, and that the smartest folk from the world he no longer haunted came from time to time to bring him some souvenir, along with their undying curiosity about him, was no longer enough to make up for what he had lost.

When it suffers, the vanity of a Dandy turns to something close to pride, and becomes as dumb as shame, though no one has credited such a frivolous man with such self-restraint. Not knowing, perhaps, how to occupy his now useless faculties, he threw himself into a correspondence with the Duchess of York, painting for her benefit a complex scene whose figures he invented. At Belvoir, at Oaklands, everywhere the Duke and Duchess had lavished their favours on him, yet since fate

leaving. The writers and artists, whose function it is to revive the feelings of others, and at the very least to sprinkle around a little of the gold dust of their work, are as unimpressive in society as mediocre folk. Exhausted from thinking all day (or from pretending to think) they go there in the evenings to relax by listening to the kind of music that makes them fall into a dream, like fakirs, or to take tea like Chinese. I know of only a single exception ...

Brummell came to Paris, but didn't stay. What would he have done there? He no longer possessed the luxury that would have made him charming, even if he had been as stupid and ugly as the Prince T... All he had was a style which was losing its meaning a little more every day. Parisians would have understood nothing about the past of such a man, and Paris would have made a sad impression on him, just as he would have made a sad spectacle for others! Mme Guiccioli made a similar spectacle of herself, even though she was a woman, and in the case of women there is always an element of nervous deference to the sex.

had betrayed him the Duchess had shown feelings towards him that cast a glow of genuine tenderness on this brilliant but arid life.*

Brummell never forgot her. It even appears that, had it not been for the friendship of the Duchess of York, to whom he had promised not to reveal what he knew about the intimate life of the Regent, he would have written his memoirs as a

---

* *This is a curious sentiment. Friendship does not exist between women (hardly an original thought, but the truth never is), a Dandy has something of the woman about him, and when he ceases to be womanly he becomes worse for a woman than women themselves, namely one of those monsters whose head is given preference to their hearts. A hateful thing, even in friendship. In Dandyism there is something cold, sober, mocking, and although it is well under control it can be instantly mobilised, which must come as an immense shock to those over-dramatic tear machines for whom the display of tender emotions is more than tenderness itself. Odious as Puritanism is to them, in extreme youth it shocks them less, and grave young men are pleasing to very young women. Duped by their serious pose, which is often accompanied by a shyness which becomes the more strained the more it seeks to pass unnoticed, they dream of profundity while facing emptiness.*

Confronted with the lightness of mind of a Dandy they dream of lightness of another sort, the kind mothers talk about, with pinched noses, before their daughters. Yet despite this — and perhaps because of it, since women are easily dominated by those they do not dominate — they can very easily be in love with an intolerable Dandy, for we can generally fall in love with anyone in this life. But here it is only friendship, which is to say a sentiment which has more to do with choice than with attraction.

way of restoring his fortune. The London booksellers were offering him immense sums as the price of his indiscretion. This silence (a most considerate one, whether it was the Duchess who made him keep it or whether he kept it voluntarily) did him little good in the eyes of that thick-skinned egotist, George IV.

It is true that when he passed through Calais on a visit to his kingdom in Hanover in 1821, in the indolence of his indifference he allowed those around him to make arrangements for a reconciliation. Brummell lent himself only half-heartedly to these official manoeuvres. Since vanity never deserts us, even when we are racked on the wheel, he did not want to ask for an audience with a Prince who was a most inferior Dandy to the one he felt himself to be. To be placed in George's path was painful for him, but he forced himself to stand there. His old associate at Carlton House saw him, but showed none of the emotion one feels when coming across a youthful companion — the cheerful regret for the past, that poetic feeling familiar to the simplest folk.

On another occasion, when the Prince was offered a snuff box he knew to have formed part of Brummell's famous collection, he asked that he should be presented to him and fixed the time of the reception for the following day. What would have happened had they met? Would the King of Calais, as Brummell was called, have returned to reign over London? But the next day dispatches arrived that forced George IV to advance his departure, and Brummell was totally forgotten.

His lack of eagerness for the encounter was at least equal to the Prince's indifference. From the point of view of the politics of life, this indolent distaste for advancing himself in the eyes of the King of England was a mistake, but if he had not committed it he would have been less the man he was.* After that George IV never again spoke about the Dandy he had glimpsed at Calais, and relapsed into oblivion about the past. Brummell did not complain, maintaining the firm and discreet silence that is the good taste of pride. And yet the events that were to follow would have given cause to many recriminations in a weaker soul. Very soon the resources from England were exhausted; then came the debts and the misery. He was about to commence the descent of that stairway of exile in poverty of which Dante spoke, and at whose bottom he was to find prison, the almshouse and the madhouse where he would die.

The hand that stopped him on the first steps of this terrible descent was a royal one, that of William IV, whose government created a post of consul at Caen and awarded it to him. Meagerly rewarded at the beginning, the position finally disappeared altogether, wound up because of

---

* *One thinks of the wonderful verses in Sardanapalus:*

> *If ... thou feel'st an inward shrinking from*
> *This leap through flame into the future, say it;*
> *I shall not love thee less, nay perhaps more,*
> *For, yielding to thy nature ...*

Brummell's disdainful incapacity* to discharge it.†

Later they took it from him. Governments are supposed to classify people according to their capacities, and when they place them in completely unsuitable posts, do they think they have done something for them? The time Brummell spent in Caen was one of the longest phases of his life. The welcome and respect afforded him by the Nobility of the town is a reminder that the ancestors of the English were Normans — a fact that softened but could not spare him the anguish of his final days.

Mr Jesse has made a careful tally of these indignities, these sufferings: as for ourselves, we shall say nothing. Why recount them? What concern us are the Dandy, his influence and his public life, his social role. What does the rest matter? When one is dying of hunger society has no time for you. You cease to be a Dandy‡ and fall back into normal life.

* *Disdainful impossibility would be fairer.*

† *He needed people to seduce, and they gave him affairs to regulate. If his capriciousness and the intense happiness of the first half of his life had not rendered him unsuitable for everything to do with public functions, perhaps there was something of the diplomat in him that could have been put to use. Perhaps: we do not press the point. Lord Palmerston has shown all too well what can happen to Dandies in politics when they find themselves isolated. Henry de Marsay is an engaging fantasy, but it is a destiny contrived by a poet. We are not saying he is an impossible figure, just that he is the less plausible hero for a novel.*

‡ *But did he cease to be one forever? One day in Caen a Venetian, content at the time to be the Casanova of music but who was later to*

We shall leave matters there. Yet to give Brummell his due, he remained a Dandy as long as a man can in poverty and hunger, and for a long time his most salient faculty lived on amongst the ruins of his life. Other sides of him, which existed merely in its support and in harmony with it, could do nothing for his fame and not very much for his contentment. For example he was a poet, with just enough imagination for a man whose vocation in life had been to please, but what he left in the way of verses, though remarkable in a Dandy, did not suggest that he was a real writer.* So we do not have to trouble ourselves with them. In this study of a man who was in his way so unusual, everything that forms no part of his role in life, of the touch of God in his intelligence, should be left aside.

* *Mr Jesse, whom we shall henceforth have to invoke when speaking of Brummell, quoted some of the verses by the celebrated Dandy in his book. Brummell inscribed them in a pretty album where Sheridan, Byron, and even Erskine had written theirs. They are not album verses, a few lines traced in haste, but quite extensive pieces with a certain whiff of inspiration.*

become its Gustave Planche — M. P. Scudo, presently with the Revue des Deux Mondes — gave one of those concerts in which, as mimic and as musician, he displayed a wit that was enough to give even imbeciles lock-jaw, if imbeciles were sentient creatures. He wanted to have at his soirée the exiled Dandy who was still a power in the Rue Guillebert. Meeting him at the house of a friend, he extended the invitation, pulled a bunch of tickets from his pocket (about three hundred), and was opening them like a pack of cards to offer him several when, in an act of appropriation and with the simplicity of a dandy to whom the world belongs, Brummell snapped them all up, with a single gesture! "He never paid me" said M. Scudo, "but the thing was admirably done, and I had for my money one more idea of what England is about."

It was not long after this incident that Brummell went mad. And since his Dandyism was stronger than his reason, and had penetrated the whole man, his madness was stamped with Dandyism. He had the rage of elegance in despair. He no longer raised his hat in the street when he was greeted, for fear of unsettling his wig, and returned the greeting with his hand in the manner of Charles X. At the time he was living in the Hôtel d'Angleterre, and some days, to the astonishment of the hotel staff, he would order his rooms to be prepared as though for a party. Chandeliers, candelabra, candles, flowers everywhere, nothing was wanting.

And there was Brummell himself, beneath all these lights, dressed to the nines as in his youth, in his blue Whig costume with the gold buttons, the quilted waistcoat and black trousers, tight as a pair of sixteenth-century breeches, in the middle of it all, waiting ... Waiting for an England that was no more! Suddenly, as though assuming a different identity, he would announce in a high tone the Prince of Wales, then Lady Connyngham, then Lord Yarmouth, in fact all the distinguished persons of England for whom he had once been a living law. And thinking that he saw them appear as he called their names he would change his voice and go to receive them at the wide open double doors of this empty salon, through which no one alas! was to pass that evening, and there he would greet them, these chimeras of his mind.

Then he would offer his arm to the ladies amongst these ghosts he had summoned up, and who would certainly not have wished to leave their tombs for an instant to attend the fallen Dandy's rout. This went on for some time. Then, when the whole place was full of ghosts, a host of worldly people who had arrived from another world, the unfortunate man would return to his senses and become conscious of his illusion and his delirium. And then he would fall, overwrought, into one of the empty chairs, and be discovered in tears!

In the hospice Le Bon Sauveur his fits of insanity were not so touching. His sickness got worse, and took a form of degradation that seemed a revenge for the elegance of his life. It is impossible to recount ... What a terrible irony that the great Railleur at the bottom of everything should end up by having his say, even in the lives of those who mocked him most! The pavilion of the Bon Sauveur was Brummell's penance for the Brighton pavilion, for his life had passed from one to the other.

XII

We now know what this role was and how he filled it. He was born to rule by qualities that were extremely practical, even if Montesquieu described them, in a fit of pique, as a *je ne sais quoi,* instead of telling us what they are. It was this that put him at the forefront of his era. As the Prince de Ligne would have said, "He was king by the grace of grace." But only on condition — and it is one that weighs on all those who trace the influence of men on others — that we accept the prejudices of the time and even to an extent its vices. For chaste friends of the truth in everything it is a sad confession to make: that if his grace had been more sincere it would have been less potent, and he would never have seduced and captivated a society lacking a taste for unaffected things.

At what degree of civilised refinement and secret corruption must English society have arrived for it to become a just and profound observation to say of a Dandy like

Brummell: *he displeased too generally not to be sought after?* *

It reminds one of the wish of powerful and debauched women to be beaten, does it not? Would grace that was simple, naive, spontaneous be a strong enough stimulant to move a world exhausted by sensation and strangulated by prejudice of every kind? If one were to remain entirely oneself in such a milieu, what sort of person would one be? Someone who was appreciated only by one or two elite souls who had remained healthy and great.† In a word, a most uncertain public!

So it is that we become vain and desirous of the approbation of others — a movement of the heart that has its charm and which has been too often criticised. That is perhaps the whole explanation of Dandyism's affectations. In the last resort it is nothing more than a form of grace which has been falsified in order that it should be better appreciated in a false society.‡ And in this sense it becomes the most natural form

* *Bulwer, in Pelham.*

† *Like for example Miss Cornel, the actress so praised by Stendhal. But to recognise the simple grandeur of her soul, rare as a black diamond in London, it needed a Stendhal. Which is to say a man with a spirit so witty and positive as to be Machiavellian, but who liked unaffected people in the same way that certain Roman emperors liked the impossible.*

‡ *The English lack an instinct for the fine arts. The names of people like Laurence, Romney, Reynolds and several others only highlight this famine. The Roman people were not artists because they had flute players. In England the only art is literature. Their*

of behaviour, well and truly compromised, certainly, but nevertheless enduring.

At the start of this work we said that the day that the society which produced Dandyism was transformed, Dandyism would be no more. Despite the tenacity of its attachment to its old customs, which resembles a fatal bondage, aristocratic and Protestant England has already greatly changed these twenty years, and Dandyism has proved to be scarcely more than the tradition of a day. Who would have believed it — or rather who could not have foreseen it? The change followed a predictable course. A victim as always of her history, after taking a step towards the future, England has resumed her seat in her past.

High as she sails on the seas of time, like the Corsaire of her greatest poet, she never quite breaks the hawser that ties her to the shore. For she who keeps everything, holds onto everything, *marble to retain*, custom becomes a strange form of enslavement. For her the seventh skin of the serpent always resembles the first she sloughed off. For a moment one

Michelangelo is Shakespeare. Since everything is special in this highly original country, the best sculptor it has produced was a woman, Lady Hamilton, who was worthy of being Italian. She sculpted in the marble pose of her own body, the most beautiful that ever breathed, a strange sort of carver of statues who was herself a statue, and whose chef d'oeuvre died with her. Her fame was one that did not outlast the brief tremblings of life and the ardent emotions of a few days! Another page that begs to be written, but where shall we find someone with Diderot's pen to do it?

believes that all traces of what has vanished have gone. Then something happens that causes the writing on the palimpsest to reappear — readable, in a firm hand, brilliant.

Today the Puritanism against which Dandyism, armed with the light arrows of its mockery, conducted a Parthian war — fleeing it rather than attacking from the front — is once more rising to its feet and binding its wounds. After Byron, after Brummell — very different satirists of the established order but who can perhaps be said to have exercised an equal influence — who would not have believed that the old Anglican morality was completely worn out? Well, it isn't, it is still there. Cant — invincible, immortal — has once again won the day. Charming fantasy can do no more than sacrifice its rose-red blood to the skies, as it succumbs to the stubbornness of a people who are the indomitable slaves of habit, and who lack great writers to electrify the imagination and inspire them with every audacity,* and finally to the influence on high society of a young queen who makes a show of conjugal love in the way Elizabeth I once did of virginity. What better sources of hypocrisy and spleen? Methodism, which once spread from public morality into politics, is currently spreading from politics to morality. Is it not the case that Lord John Manners, a poet with a fine pedigree who inherited from birth the very easy courage of having an independent

---

* *This absence is not total, since we have Thomas Carlyle. Yet what a pity he so often prefers the sedating ether of German spiritualism to the quickening caviar the English prefer, and which affords such keen sensations!*

opinion, and could expect true inspiration from his talent, has just published a volume of poetry dedicated to the established Church of England? Today the atheist Shelley would no longer be safe even in exile.

Free thought, which beamed down like a ray of intelligence from its greatest men on this country of arrogant pharisaism, of icy and mendacious convention, shone for a brief moment only, and the mummy of religious sentiment and formality still reigns in the depths of its whitened sepulchure. Everything is finished, everything is gone of this splendid society of which Brummell was the idol, because he was its expression in the things of this world, in human relations dedicated to pure pleasure. We shall never see Dandies like Brummell again. Though men like him, whatever disguise the world forces them to adapt, we can be sure there will always be, even in England.

They are proof of the magnificent variety of the divine order. They are as eternal as caprice. Humanity has as much need of them as of its most imposing heroes, and of its most austere grandeurs. It is they who give intelligent creatures the pleasure they have a right to. They represent the happiness of society in the way that other men represent its morality. Double and multiple natures, of undecided intellectual sexuality, their grace is heightened by their power, and their power by grace. They are the Hermaphrodites of History, not of Fable, of whom Alcibiades was the supreme example in the most beautiful of nations.

A Dandy before the Dandies

I

Will this study of Dandyism, and of the man who personifies it most exactly and irreducibly, suffice to give an adequate notion of something so profoundly, and so insularly English as Dandyism? English as it is, as we have seen it is nevertheless not entirely a social phenomenon — which is to say a monstrosity, as Puritans and the tender-hearted, reconciled for the occasion, might agree. Dandyism has its roots in the human nature of all countries and all times, since vanity is universal. What might be called the chord of Dandyism, one of the thirty-six thousand chords that compose that devilish instrument, so complex and sometimes so deranged, that is human nature, is at present mute, but will again resound. And it was England that made it resound most loudly!

We have cited the case of Richelieu and contrasted him with Brummell, so as to underline the difference that race and society placed between two fops constructed on the same foundations! Richelieu most certainly possessed the Dandyist chord, but its vibration was muted in him by still more powerful vibrations. Another Dandy before the Dandies like Richelieu, before Dandyism was named as such and observers brought their superfine analyses to bear on it as a thing in itself, was Lauzun, a stronger specimen than Richelieu even if he didn't take Port Mahon ... He took something better than that. It was the Great Mademoiselle and he took her all by himself, which cannot be said of Richelieu and Port Mahon. And he took her, it should be noted, above all by the Dandyism that was in him even if he didn't know it, any more than her!

Lauzun was worthy of being an Englishman. Had he been, he would have made one of the most magnificent English Dandies. He had the Englishman's egoism, the most terrible egoism that has existed since the Romans. In his dress, in his originality — a quality nuanced in his dress — in his claim to be unlike others, at a time when the others were all equal before Louis XIV, in his sangfroid, his self-control, the element of unexpectedness in his behaviour (one of the characteristics of the Dandy is never to do what is expected of him) Lauzun was a Dandy.

He possessed the Dandy's pitiless, tigerish vanity. Think of the scene in the memoirs of Saint-Simon, where he put his heel on the hand of a duchess (and heels were worn as high in Louis XIV's time as they are in our day, 1879) and executes a pirouette in order to drive it into her hand like a brace and bit. It is enough to make a nervous reader scream. There would be a fine story to be written about Lauzun, had it not been written already, but it has, and to make things more absurd, it was written by the princess who was more madly in love with Lauzun than any other woman. A Cesare Borgia when it came to women, especially this one, this particular Borgia, who could have shown Machiavelli a trick or two, had no need to write his Commentaries like the great Caesar himself. They were written by a woman, his conquest, a princess in love who was badly treated but remained in love. Brummell, for his part, has had as his historians only Captain Jesse and myself.

Some wonderful pages in the memoirs of Mlle de Montpensier give us the measure of Lauzun, this Dandy before the Dandies, this French Englishman. It is a tale worthy of a Stendhal novel, and this is the place, rather than elsewhere, to discuss it.

II

In her memoirs the Great Mademoiselle shows a princess's originality, something unknown in our times, and a way of feeling almost incomprehensible to our flat-footed habits and customs. Here I find something fine in the past: *pride in respect for oneself and for one's race, which is more than oneself.* She was more of a Bourbon than a woman, and I can see now how she was happy to have black teeth, since they were the teeth of her House.

Until Lauzun arrived her heart, according to her memoirs, appears to have trembled for no one. All she desired was to marry the old German emperor, simply because he was emperor. Courted by the King of England (Charles II was in France at the time) she took no notice. She looked on calmly as all the houses of cards people constructed around her marriage collapsed; her only preoccupation was that a daughter of France should not be sold too cheap! If she dreamt, as is said, of her own cousin, Louis XIV, nothing is breathed in the memoirs. Pride imposes silence on pride.

This princess in the fullest sense, this soul that was moved by nothing except etiquette, this ceremonial being who aimed at nothing but grandeur — the grandeur of the theatre and of esteem (honour, for Montesquieu) — when she was coming up to forty-three, felt her head spin with excitement for a man. The fruit is ripe ... A forty-three-year-old virgin! A virgin in everything, even perhaps in curiosity, what a passion this must be, especially when recounted by Herself! A tremendous book, surely, and for connoisseurs, it is.

III

Here we are far removed from the cynicism of Rousseau and the frankness of the times, yet see how naive she is in her own way. She has the truth of pride. She exaggerates the virtues of the man she loves simply because she loves him. But she does not go beyond exaggeration. It was obviously impossible that, to her eyes, the man for whom, at forty-three, she was to feel this love for which nothing in her life had prepared her, was not superior to all others. And at the court of the great king, young and splendid at the time like a May sun, it was hard to excel others in wit, manners, and beauty. But in this century of Convention where everything is alike, the superiority of Lauzun is extraordinary: it is what we would call today, since the word did not exist at the time, originality. Before falling in love with him at a tournament, Mademoiselle is struck by Lauzun's air (at the time he was the Count of Peguylem), and by his proud device: a rocket soaring into the clouds and bearing the motto: *I shall rise as high as man can.* She thought it unusual, which indeed it was.

Before being a captain in the guards Lauzun had been a colonel of dragoons, whose caps, she said, "indicated a kind of bravura in this troop *that one did not see in others* ..." "Their colonel", she continued, "appeared with an air which distinguished him all the more from *other* officers in that he did so on occasions where they would have been hard put to imitate him. He was *extraordinary* in everything ... Finding him to be a man of wit I would have liked to speak to him at once, so touched was I by his reputation of being an honest and *unusual* man. He was *special.* He communicated with few people. I knew this more from others than from myself." When he was named a captain of guards, he took the baton and exercised the function "with a fine, easy air" she said, "with great solicitude but without eagerness, and I began to see him as an extraordinary man" (it was always the greatest impression he made on her), "very agreeable in conversation, and I sought opportunities to speak with him. In him I found a way of expressing himself that I did not find in *others*."

Such was the first spell cast by this charmer! In this great century of Convention, we sense nothing in the marbled heart of a princess that would be called in the succeeding century love at first sight. People were not highly strung and the magnetism of a look was unknown. Bit by bit Lauzun imposed himself in the attentions of this bored woman, who probably found, perhaps without noticing, that at this solemn court everything resembled everything else. And since, princess or not, one still has one's female vanity, the ladies' man in Lauzun insinuated itself, needle-like, into this proud blood. Speaking of Henrietta of England, Duchess of Orléans, she says: "I had no suspicion that he could have had galant feelings towards her ... *the kind of attachment it was normal for him to have for many women.*"

At this point she begins to see into her heart. "God" (she says with the gravity of Bossuet) "is the master of our station in life. He leaves to us as much as the vanity of our spirits can suffer. If he had permitted me to see my own state as the happiest that I could want in the world, I should be satisfied with my birth, my welfare, etc etc. However, as I have said, I was bored in places where I had taken pleasure before, without knowing the reason ..." So it starts, as it must, with boredom: *"God, you have made me powerful and solitary!"*

"I became fond of people towards whom I had formerly been indifferent ... I liked M. de Lauzun's conversation even when it left no trace in my mind." How slow everything is in a soul which has so much trouble in relaxing! *"After spending a long time* in these agitations", she goes on, "I wanted to escape into myself and ask what gave me pleasure and what gave me pain. I knew that another *condition* than that which I had experienced till then had taken hold of me entirely: that if I were married I would be happier: that to make someone's fortune, to give him great establishments would please him, he would be touched, he would feel friendly towards me and would apply himself to doing everything to please me ..." And after all this self-examination, with its flavour of Bossuet, she names Lauzun, still called M. de Lauzun, and what decides her in his favour is above all "the distinctions of his behaviour *compared with that of others,* the elevation of his soul above that of *other people*, the pleasure of his conversation and *a million singularities* that I have discerned in him ..."

Always the singularities, the originality, the extraordinary, the unforeseen for her, in her routine of the high life of a princess. She had divined modern Dandyism, this woman, for clearly Dandyism is what it is.

IV

Mathilde de la Mole, in *Le Rouge et le Noir*, is as well aware of her feelings as Mademoiselle. Only Mathilde puts up a struggle, whereas Mademoiselle is too much a princess to struggle against her feelings. If that is what she feels, so be it! Ennui grips her when she *doesn't find him* in the Queen's apartments. "I wanted to see him with the Queen, or *alone*, in my room, or at court, be it by accident, or *otherwise*. I am naturally impatient, and could suffer no one's company. Society puts me in a state of despair ..."

No sooner are these powerful symptoms registered, than two feelings are born. First, a resolve to declare her love to the King, together with her *inconsolability* at the idea that Lauzun, respectful and deferential in his behaviour, did not appear to have noticed how much her thoughts were on him. Still very much the princess, however, and *agitated* as she is, she is much taken with examples from French history of people less elevated than Lauzun who had married the daughters or even the widows of kings. She remembers the loves of Corneille and — a strange thing — sends to Paris for an edition of his works, because she recalls (she says) someone in one of his plays who shared a fate not dissimilar to her own. When the works arrived, she got by heart the verses she had remembered only indistinctly, seeing in a godly light, she hastens to add, what most people consider with profane feelings. Here are Corneille's rather splendid verses:

When divine dispensation made us one for another,
Lisa, our love is one that is soon realised.
By a secret power its hand sows the knowledge before
they meet!
So well does it prepare the lover and his mistress
That their souls are excited at the other's very name.
They value each other, seek each other, love each other in
an instant.
Everything they say to one another is easily
comprehensible.

Freed from the anxieties of a thousand petty fears
Trust seems to run ahead of their words.
Their tongues say many things in few words.
Their eyes, more eloquent, make everything instantly
                                                    visible,
And whatever it is the two of them vie to tell us,
The heart understands more than the two of them say!

Once the genius has spoken his oracle, she hesitates no more. Her purpose is fixed, and she takes her marriage plans right up to the Saint-Sacrement. One day, a second of March, she sees Lauzun with the Queen. "When I was before him he must have guessed how much my heart went out to him," she says, "by the gaiety with which I talked to him." But since Lauzun, under cover of his respect, does not seem to understand anything, she pretends to discuss with him a marriage with the Duc of Lorraine, and to ask for his advice ...

And this is where the most delicious comedy, the comedy of love, begins. She wants him to understand and he — who understands perfectly well — does not wish to at all. She holds out to him the ice she has split, so that he can finish breaking it. It is no more than a weak, transparent surface but he doesn't break it. He does not even lay a finger on it, and if he did his touch would be enough to shatter it. Lauzun becomes the most gracious, the most profound, the most infuriating Tartuffe of respect there has ever been. The behaviour of this man is a chef-d'oeuvre. Axioms and maxims about how to make princesses fall in love with you can be drawn from it. The trouble is, where are the princesses to be seduced today? There are women who have the title, but the princess spirit exists no more.

The first axiom of Lauzun's beguiling machiavellism, for the details are indeed beguiling, is as follows. The more a proud woman, a princess in spirit as well as birth, becomes tender and diaphanous, the thicker one's respect for her should be, and the more impenetrably one should wrap oneself in it. Lauzun never broke this law, not even in intimate conversations that were intoxicating for someone as vain as he was, as ambitious as he was, and in love as he may have been (maybe he was? Libertines are capable of anything, even of loving a forty-three-year-old woman). In over-excited vanity there is something that is devilishly like love — and devilish is the word.

In the memoirs of the Grande Mademoiselle one reads of these tricks of respect, and of the tricks of a proud, exasperated tenderness. This princess, who takes trouble with her pen, writes some charming things, of a kind only authors of genius have written. The veiled grace and hypocritically displayed passion are wonderful — the kind of passion *which wants to be seen* but does not want to show itself ... A piquant situation! She asks for his advice. He gives her some, searches with her for someone she might marry, finds no one, gives her the idea of immersing herself in religious devotion — the devotion of time. He is magnificently grave, this man who sees quite clearly that he is adored. "It is not that I believe it to be ridiculous to pass one's entire life without taking a partner, whatever one's rank and degree", he says. "When one is forty one must not indulge in pleasures that are suitable for girls from fifteen to twenty-four. Therefore I must tell you where you should become a nun and take up your devotions." At the same time he approves her plan to elevate someone to her position, but pretends to be completely in the dark about the man on whom her eyes are fixed.

Meanwhile, in the course of Mademoiselle's love for Lauzun, Madame (the King's sister and Duchess of Orléans) dies. The King speaks of replacing her with Mademoiselle. But the friend of the Chevalier de Lorraine does not suit this suberbly feminine soul, and the King, who knows what is what, is ashamed of his idea and in the end discards it. Lauzun is the only one who, with the devilish intelligence of someone who understands women, pretends to believe that Mademoiselle desires this marriage, and advises her to accept... At this point Mademoiselle, at the end of her tether, confesses her love to Lauzun himself — though by dint of such embarrassment and blushes! This proud girl has a wonderfully childlike heart. As for him, he sticks to his system. When he is absolutely sure that she is going to tell him everything, he will not hear a word of it, and begs her to keep her counsel.

"He told me that *I had made him tremble*. 'If through some caprice I did not approve your taste', he said, 'I can see that you would never dare see me again, stubbornly determined as you are. I am too anxious to keep the honour of your good graces to hear a confidence that would risk me losing them. I will not hear of it, and I beg you not to speak another word to me of this affair ...'"

He knew exactly how to fan the flames of desire, this

incendiary! The less he wants to hear the more she wants to tell. One day, still on the same subject, she says: "I was tempted to breathe on the mirror, it would dull the glass and I would write the name in big letters so that you could read it clearly." But midnight struck. It was Friday, an inauspicious day. "Ah", she said, "I won't say another word to you." Some days later she hid in her pocket a piece of paper on which she had simply written: "It's you!" But she does not want to give it to him on a Friday. "Give it to me" Lauzun told her, "and I promise not to open it till after midnight." But she is afraid, and is still hesitating, when after dinner the next day he comes to the Queen's apartments and she writes this ravishing page in her memoirs, whose details seem to me inexpressibly charming:

"When the Queen had gone to pray, I placed myself alone with him at the corner of the fireside, took out my paper and showed it to him, then put it back in my pocket or perhaps in my sleeve. He pressed me, very strongly, to give it him. He said that his heart was beating hard, that he thought it was a forewarning that I was going to give him the opportunity to do someone a bad service, if he didn't approve of my choice and my intentions. This kind of talk went on for a good hour, but each of us was as embarrassed as the other so I said to him: here is the paper. I will give it to you on condition that you give me a reply underneath my writing. You will find plenty of space, since my note is short, and you will give it back to me this evening at the Queen's apartments where we shall speak together."

"I had hardly finished when the Queen came from her

prie-dieu to go to a convent service. I followed, praying God with all my heart for my plans to be fulfilled. I was deeply distracted. After leaving the church, we went to see the Dauphin. The Queen came close to the fire. I saw M. de Lauzun enter and approach me without daring to speak to me, or even look. His embarrassment made my own worse. I threw *myself on my knees the better to warm myself*. He was right next to me. Without looking at him I said 'I am frozen through.' He replied: 'I am still troubled by what I have seen. But I am not stupid enough to fall into your trap. I was well aware that you wanted to amuse yourself, and to stop yourself, by an extraordinary trick, from telling me the name of this person. I shall never be curious, so long as you have the slightest aversion from confessing something to me.' I replied to him: 'Nothing could be more certain than the two words I have written to you, and nothing more decided in my head than the execution of this matter.' *He did not have the time to reply, or did not find the strength to bear a longer conversation.*"

Again, the details and the tone are incomparable.

V

And this is where the deep seducer becomes admirable, more and more satanically admirable. The stroke of luck which falls on him makes no breach in the tortoiseshell of hypocrisy in which he has wrapped himself. He is indifferent to what is said to him by this enamoured noblewoman, who has not rediscovered (since she never had them) but discovered, with true feeling, the timid graces of an eighteen-year-old girl. The

"It's you!", and everything that she adds to this terrible and delicious "It's you!", does not disturb Lauzun's mask of incredulity for a moment. He tells her "she is making fun of him" and she replies, with far more justification that, on the contrary, "it is he who is making fun of her."

The roles are inverted. Normally it is the man who does the persuading, and the woman the one he wants to persuade. Here the princess is the man, and the cadet of the family, the woman. And what a woman! Celimène and Tartuffe combined! The more she pours the lustre of her royal love on his head, the smaller and more humble he makes himself. He seems to be saying to this woman who is abasing herself for him: abase yourself more! It is the opposite and justification of his device, the lucky rogue: *"I shall rise as far as any man can!"*

The facts in this novelettish comedy — a novel for her, a comedy for him — are as splendid as the novel itself. Everything is there. At this court whose etiquette borders on the Spanish, she dares to lean on him when she gets up. He uses this moment to return the paper to her, which, like a little girl, she hides in her sleeve — and this is the heroine of the Faubourg Saint-Antoine, who fired canon against Louis XIV! He stubbornly pretends not to believe it, but a light has crossed his mask, which she has seen quite clearly. "He will always" he says, "submit to her will." This is not a "no", but having said this much — and it was impossible not to say it — he then immerses himself in respect, in such a way as to drive her mad with annoyance! Finally he drops the weighty word — the word *humiliating*: "Could it be possible that you would wish to marry a servant of your cousin?" He was referring to his commission as captain in the Garde du Corps.

But, just as he had expected, every obstacle he put in Mademoiselle's path made her the more determined to leap over it. So she boldly requested the King's permission to marry M. de Lauzun. Amazingly, the King did not object. He told Mademoiselle to think about it carefully, not to act lightly, etc. Mademoiselle is pained by the intention to delay matters that she divines in the King's response, and Lauzun defends the King against her! He thinks that the King is right to tell her to reflect on something that he finds *unsuitable*, etc etc.

The King says nothing to Lauzun, he is gracious towards both him and her. This gives Mademoiselle hope, then one evening, when they are with the Queen, Lauzun says to her brusquely: "You must no longer put off talking to the King. If you take my advice you will say to him: Sire, *the briefest* follies are the best. I come to thank His Majesty for making me reflect. I *no longer think* about what I asked him." But Mademoiselle, beside herself with exasperation, speaks to the King in quite another sense, and with what tact, what taste, what resolve! (See page 24, volume VI). The King says only one thing: "I am not opposed to your wishes or to M. de Lauzun's fortune, but act only after reflection."

It was consent. The whole court learnt the astounding news: Mademoiselle is to be married! Lauzun has a modest air, blushing almost, a man to be married like a young girl. "I need all my powers of reason" he says, "to prevent me losing my head." When the marriage contract has been drawn up, and everything is ready for the ceremony, Lauzun, the same

Lauzun who has been following his logic of humility, says to Mademoiselle: "If you feel *the slightest aversion* when you are before the priest, I beg you with all my heart to break things off." To which Mademoiselle replies: *"You do not love me."* "That is something I shall only say", he says, "when I have left the church. I would rather be dead than to have you know before then what I have in my heart for you ..." At this point a sudden and immense sadness falls on her heart, on the great heart of this happy girl. *Without knowing why,* she says, she begins to cry. And the next day the King calls off the marriage!

VI

My sole concern here is with the superior fashion in which Lauzun carried out his seduction of Mademoiselle. He did it like the greatest artist in seduction ever seen. In vain have I searched his conduct for a single error, an oversight, a moment of distraction. It needed nothing less than the will of Louis XIV to overturn Lauzun's chef d'oeuvre, and a Louis XIV who was no longer himself, since this King, rightly seen as the most honest man in his kingdom, conducted himself on this occasion either with the utmost weakness or the utmost duplicity. Surrounded, pressured and pestered by the faction of Monsieur, his brother, by the mother-in-law of Mademoiselle and by her sister, who had married a de Guise, he surrendered miserably, having given Mademoiselle his consent, which would appear to be a failure to keep his word. Or did he trick her, which would be both a lie and an act of cruelty? In either case Louis XIV renders himself small and almost dishonest. The only explanation he gave the desperate Mademoiselle, who was both eloquent and pathetic at his feet, was the alleged reaction of the courts of Europe — a cowardly excuse that Mademoiselle boldly described as shameful. He was inflexible before her tears but *he cried* in refusing her. When tigers eat us they do not cry, and when crocodiles spill tears, it is to attract us. These tears of Louis XIV diminish his great countenance and remain incomprehensible, even if they are not dishonourable ...

Mademoiselle's despair was tragic. Lauzun cried, in order to make her despair even more. No doubt there was some truth in these tears. How could he not have cried? Boabdil cried over his town. The King, still odious, came to Mademoiselle to console her, kissed her and for a long time held his cheek close to hers. Mademoiselle was brave enough to say: "You are behaving like those monkeys who smother their children with their caress", a phrase almost as bold as her famous canon shot!

In her anguish Mademoiselle decided no longer to appear at court. It was Lauzun who forced her back again, saying it was wrong to remain distant from the King for so long. When she met Lauzun she cried, wherever it was. The man of steel, who used this steel to rend the heart of this princess even more in the service of the passion that he inspired in her, went so far as to say to her: "*If you go on like this, I shall never be where you are. I shall stay in my room.*" After which she says she never again dared to cry in his presence!

After the marriage was called off, the King awarded Lauzun a governorship, which drew from Mademoiselle the comment: "I shall never be content with what the King does until he has given me to you. Until then all your promotions will mean nothing to me." Now that his wedding was off, Lauzun affected to neglect his dress,* which *increased the chagrin* of Mademoiselle, but he *demanded* that she take good care of *her*s, despite an affliction which made her thinner. She loved him with a physical idolatry without which there is no love. (For example, the charming story of the rose-coloured ribbon on Lauzun's cravat, at the parade for the departure to Flanders, in volume IV of the memoirs.) Even after the wedding was called off, the poor woman endlessly suffered the outrageous cruelties with which Lauzun attached to himself, as if by nails, her spellbound heart. One day there was a rumour that she was going to marry the Duke of York. He went to her and said: "If you want to marry the Duke of York, I shall ask the King to send me to England to negotiate the marriage." And she replied, sublimely: "Only to you!" On hearing these words he threw himself at her feet and

---

* *More likely, he did it on purpose. His dress must have been as hypocritical as his conduct. He was not a man to pour ashes on his head like a Jew in his affliction, and if he did, it was a mere sprinkling. Only a light powdering of sadness which does not spoil one's looks and makes one appear interesting. Lauzun was too much of a natural Dandy to overlook external effects. That is what preoccupies them. Remember the Russian Dandy in Stendhal's Le Rouge et le Noir who recommends that Julien Sorel wears a melancholy black tie whenever he gives the maid of the woman he loves the famous letters to which she never replies ...*

remained there in silence. "I was tempted to lift him up", she says, "but I overcame this desire, and he got up on his own and left."

He went to Flanders, affecting to forget to say goodbye to this woman whose life he took with him. She reproached him, but says, "I wanted to be angry with him, but when I saw him I no longer had the strength!" She really was infatuated. "Sometimes", she goes on, "I felt like complaining and scolding him, but he took away my desire to do so *in ways that I find it hard to describe*, so singular are they." Always this singularity! Always this Dandyism!

VII

I repeat, my sole concern today has been with this seduction by Lauzun, which is something special in the history of human seductions. I have no need therefore to speak of his arrest and his imprisonment in the fortress of Pignerol ... Mademoiselle remained seduced by him till her final day, and the scorn she was later to feel for him had no effect on his ascendancy. He was let out of Pignerol. He went to Bourbon, then to Amboise, and finally returned to the court. He came back without disguise. He no longer hoped for marriage and the seduction was accomplished. Now he showed himself in his true colours, as a gambler, a libertine, a religious hypocrite, greedy, lacking in pride, and with no gratitude towards Mademoiselle, at a time when he was deceiving her and showing anger against her. All this is appalling. But what power! Mademoiselle sees everything, knows everything, "but I had done too much not to bring to an end what I had begun." It was the fate of pride in love.

And she achieved her end. Finally Louis XIV allowed a secret marriage, but at what price? At the price of half Mademoiselle's fortune, ceded to one of his bastards! Alas! he continued, in this story of Mademoiselle and Lauzun, not to be Louis XIV! The memoirs do not reach this point. They are suddenly discontinued, as if from shame! But the reader can already hear in the distance the words which rang across centuries: "Henriette de Bourbon, take these boots off for me!", said to the cousin of the proudest king who ever existed.

You must agree that this story, which is no more than an episode in the history of the Dandy who is to come, is as enthralling as any novel dreamt up in our times, and far more interesting to analyse!

APPENDIX TO THE SECOND EDITION

This book only just managed a second edition. Published in no more than a few copies, not many years ago it was being passed from hand to hand amongst a few people, and this form of intimate and abstruse publicity appears to have brought it luck. Will the greater publicity we hope for today be equally beneficial? Fame, a light thing, is like women: it comes to you just when you look as if you were running away. In this devilish world maybe the best way of *making one's name* would be through organised indiscretions.

But the author was not such a deep fellow when he published this bauble. At the time he didn't pay much attention to literary fame or to literary affairs. Ah yes, he had other toilettes to make besides the one of his mind, and other concerns besides that of being read! Not that he gives a damn about what mattered to him at the time, because that is how life is. Does it not all lie in this exchange, endlessly repeated, between something you once cared about and your later derision for it? The author of *On Dandyism and George Brummell* was not a Dandy (for reasons the reader will discover from this book), but he was at that stage of his youth which made Lord Byron say, with his melancholy irony, "When I was a curly-haired beau ...", and at that moment fame itself was not worth a single one of those curls!

Therefore he wrote without authorly pretensions — don't worry, he had others, the devil had his due — this very small book, purely for his own pleasure and that of thirty people, unknown friends, on whom one is not sure one can rely, which in Paris one can hardly boast of having without being conceited. Since he was not lacking in conceit he believed that he had them, and he did. Allow him to say, since he has become rather modest, that he had his thirty readers for his thirty copies. This was not the Combat, but the sympathy of the Thirty!

If the book had been about some great theme or some great man, doubtless it would have sunk from sight, with its handful of copies, in that silence of inattention that is due and is invariably paid to what is great by what is small. But it was about a frivolous man, one who had passed for the most accomplished type of frivolous elegance in a recalcitrant society. Nowadays everyone in society thinks of himself as elegant, or aspires to be ... Even those who have given up trying at the very least want to be experts in the matter, and that was why the book was read. Fools, whom I shall not name, flattered themselves they had understood it. For my part, I told my editor they would buy it. Conceit all round! The conceit that made the initial success of this small thing — on whose first page there was a temptation to write impudently: "From a fop, by a fop, for other fops." — will also make the second. For to a fop everything is a looking glass, and for them this book is a mirror. Many will come to look at themselves in it and comb their moustache, some to recognise themselves there, others to make themselves out as Brummells!

Clearly they will be wasting their time. One doesn't make oneself into a Brummell. One either is one or one is not. Futile sovereign of a futile world, Brummell has his divine right and his claim to be like other kings. Now that, in recent times, we have given all manner of idlers to think they are sovereign, why should not the population of the salons have their illusions, like those of the street?

All the more since this little book will cure them of their illusion. Here they will see that Brummell was the rarest of individuals, who not only took the trouble to be born, but who needed, to develop, the benefits of a highly complicated aristocratic society. Here they will see just how much it takes to be a Brummell, which they do not possess! The author of *On Dandyism* has tried to sum up those small but potent things by which one dominates not only women, but he was well aware as he did it that his book was not a manual, and that Machiavellis of elegance could be even sillier than political Machiavellis, who are silly enough! In a word he was aware that this was no more than a sliver of history, an archeological fragment, suitable for placing as a curiosity on the gilded toilettes of future fops — assuming they have them. For Progress, with its political economy and territorial divisions, is in the process of turning humankind into a race of vermin. It will not destroy fops, but it could destroy their d'Orsay-type toilettes, as scandalously inegalitarian.

In any event here is the book such as it was written. Nothing has been changed, and nothing deleted. All the author has done is to sharpen up a few of the notes here and there. The gravity of the times, which often makes him laugh, has not affected him to the point where he sees this little book, light of tone as it is (he is happy enough with that, doesn't find it distasteful) as a wild oat of his youth for which he feels obliged to apologise. He would even be capable, at a pinch, of insisting to the biggest cuckolds amongst these grave gentlemen that his book is as serious as any other historical tome. For what does one find here, in its brief sparkling light? Man and his vanity, social refinement and effects that are very real, though incomprehensible to Reason alone, that hugely stupid woman, but all the more attractive for being difficult to understand and hard to penetrate. What can be more serious than this, even from the superior point of view of those who have turned themselves from the world, from all its pomp and its works, and who have derided its nullity the most? Ask them! Are not all vanities the same to their eyes, under whatever name they go by and whatever their pretences? If Dandyism had existed in his time Pascal, a man with a six-horse carriage, and a Dandy insofar as one can be in France, could perhaps have written its history before entering Port-Royal. And before submerging himself in his Trappist jungle, Rance, another tiger of austerity, could perhaps have translated Captain Jesse for us, instead of Anacreon. For Rance too was a Dandy, a preacher-Dandy, which is better than a Dandy mathematician. And look at the influence of Dandyism! Dom Gervaise, a weighty, religious fellow who wrote the Life of Rance, has left us a charming description of his delicious costumes, as if he wanted to give us credit for resisting temptation by giving us a terrible desire to wear them!

Not that the author of *On Dandyism* sees himself as a Pascal, or a Rance. He has and never will be a Jansenist, and till now is no Trappist!

J.A. Barbey d'Aurevilly

INDEX